Define Your Inner Diva

Turn your mid-life crisis into a mid-life REVOLUTION

KERRY HOWARD
Psychologist

DEFINE YOUR INNER DIVA
First published in Australia in 2017 by
Diva Publications
a wholly owned subsidiary of
Ms Pink Enterprises Pty Ltd
10 Euroka Street
Narrabundah ACT 2604

National Library of Australia Cataloguing-in-Publication entry

Creator: Howard, Kerry A., 1969-author
Title: Define your inner diva: turn your mid-life crisis into a mid-life revolution / Kerry Howard
ISBN: 9780995425125: paperback
9780995425156: paperback: POD
9780995425163: paperback: POD
9780995425132: ebook: epub
9780995425149: ebook: kindle
Includes bibliographical references and index
Subjects: Single Women—Life skills guides
Women—conduct of life
Self-actualization (Psychology) in women

Cover design by Designerability

www.kerryannhoward.com
www.mspinkherself.com

Author Acknowledgements

For my daughters
Stephanie and Elysha

Steph – for being the lovely, supportive, understanding and fabulous individual that you have become.

Elysha – for being the wonderfully inspiring and unique person that you are.

There are many family and friends, colleagues, clients and acquaintances that I could acknowledge here, but I simply don't have the space and you would all be really bored reading the list anyway.

I want to acknowledge the support of a number of individuals who have been with me on this journey in big and small ways in the writing and production of this book.

Deb – for providing me a nice little 'holiday spot' in which I could focus on my writing @ Deb's Beach House in Hurghada, Egypt.

Ceri – for always being available to bounce ideas around with me and for being the most 'amazing' financial planner the world has known.

Lizzy – for being the first to 'review' and provide me feedback on the manuscript. Your input was truly valuable and helped me turn this into a truly unique and inspiring workbook.

Montse – for always believing in me and being my 'wife', the person I can unload to about EVERYTHING including the joys of publishing.

I'm so grateful that in the Divorce, I got to keep you.

Marcus – for providing me with the much needed backing to go through this process and see it through until the end. No matter how our paths diverge, know that I am forever grateful to you for your support. You allowed me the space to be ME!

Mum – for giving me life, teaching me the value of education through your actions and being the best role model of a 'fempowered' woman that I know.

About this book

Define Your Inner Diva meets the growing demand for simple, practical and effective advice for professional, single women to better understand themselves and clearly define what they seek in life, as well as providing guidance on how to be healthy, find successful and supportive relationships and live luscious lives.

The value of understanding ourselves is not always clear in relation to how we treat ourselves, how we interact with others, or how we find our best balance in order to feel that life is fun, enriching and fulfilling.

This book will resolve the issues that currently exist within the self-help industry, which focuses on individual problems and doesn't provide a comprehensive review and exploration process by which successful women can understand why they have been able to achieve career satisfaction, but not achieve optimal health, full meaning in life, or find their most supportive life partners.

As a psychologist and executive coach, author Kerry Howard, also known as Ms Pink Herself, provides direction and understanding based on her knowledge of human behaviour. Her approach in this book is unique due to its semi-autobiographical nature; it is peppered with her experiences in applying this information to her own life. Kerry has made this journey herself and assisted over 500 others to do so as well. This book comes from a place of practical experience and credibility across all forms of personal transformation.

Kerry provides down-to-earth advice for professional women on every aspect of the life review process from self, relationships, career, finances, health and wellbeing and spirit. *Define Your Inner Diva* is the answer for those women who have always wanted to be truly happy, focused on their health and satisfied in their bodies, who seek to gain a supportive partner who loves and respects their unique value and contribution to the world.

"Kerry Howard is insightful, inspirational and amazingly intuitive in understanding the 'secret' desires of fabulous professional women"

Christina Sanchez, Business In Heels

"Kerry is passionate about empowering women to let go of their doubts and limitations and embrace their fullest potential!"

Lisa LaMaitre,
Canberra Wise Women

"For many years I have tried to be what others wanted me to be, this kind of daughter, that kind of wife… But thanks to Ms Pink, now I am learning to be ME."

Tammie, 47yo Executive,
Divorced, 3 Adult Daughters

If you have always wanted to love your whole life, and make it an awesome existence full of fun, food and love, then this is the book for you.

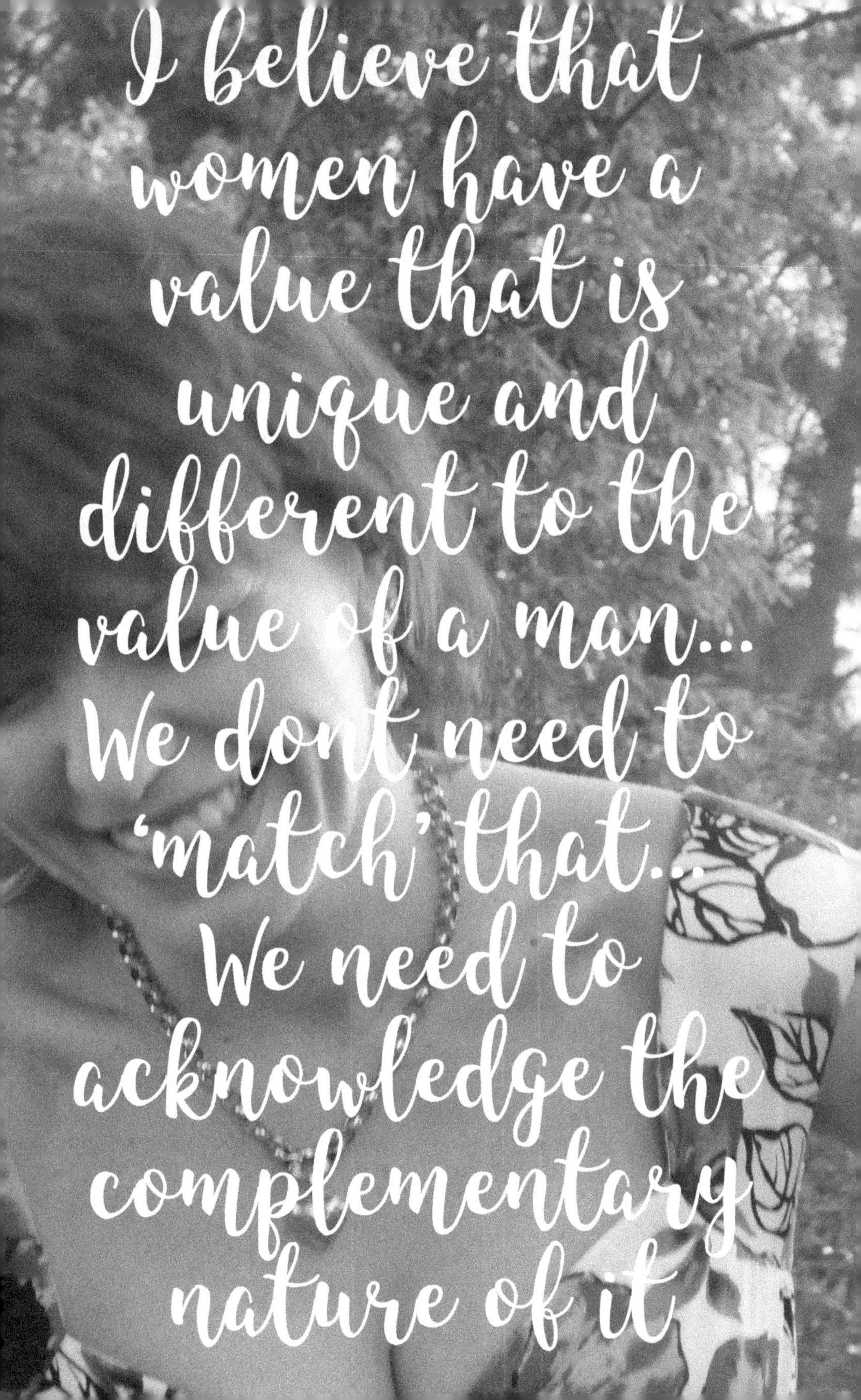

I believe that women have a value that is unique and different to the value of a man... We dont need to 'match' that... We need to acknowledge the complementary nature of it

Preface

From the outset I want you to know why I wrote this book. I have a burning desire to share the knowledge of self-improvement with as many women as I can. Not because I know better, but because I want to share what I have learned throughout my life and hope you can engage with me in my journey and see how this may provide insight into your own journey.

This book covers all aspects of life – your sense of self, relationships, career, finances, health and wellbeing and your spirit. It outlines why we need to make changes in our lives so that we can greet each day with gratitude, allowing us to live our lives full of 'Awesome!'

What this book isn't...

It is important to understand that I have written this as an overview workbook; it is designed to highlight the things that we need to consider changing and the importance of those things, but it does not provide all of the answers – simply because it can't.

We are all individuals, with different backgrounds and different goals for our futures. One book may be able to highlight what needs to be done to improve things, the issues that need to be considered, but it cannot provide an in-depth explanation of how to fully implement those changes – that is why I work with individuals with the varying areas that I overview in this book.

What this book is...

In working through this book, we become much more aware of why we face certain issues in life and this creates clarity around what needs to happen if we want to change things for the better.

As this has been designed as a practical workbook, there are multiple assessments and review processes that I will ask you to complete throughout the book. However, it is neither practical nor aesthetically appealing to have all of these processes outlined in this book, so I will regularly refer you to my website to engage with more content. I apologise in advance if this is annoying, but it is more efficient. The bonus of online assessments is that you don't have to do the scoring!

By the end of this book, you will have a clear outline of the aspects that you want to improve in each area of your life and insights into how you might move forward in resolving any issues. It is an individual plan for your future.

Who am I?

I am a 'fempowered' woman! One who embraces the *feminine* and has lived a full and *empowered* life. The youngest of five children, raised in a sole parent household, I grew up on the wrong side of the tracks. I left school at 16 and worked briefly before realising that the ONLY way I was going to get what I wanted for myself in this life was through education. So, from the time I left school until I graduated with my psychology degree at the age of 40, I continuously studied part-time whilst working. It was not always formal education, but I was always learning.

I am a woman who has been married twice, the first time at just 21, and has had two awful Family Court cases. As a sole parent raising two gorgeous girls, I tried to maintain a social life while studying part-time and working full-time.

I am a woman who has struggled with her weight, from a family of women with similar weight issues. After many years of yo-yoing with my weight, I lost 40kgs. I proudly say that I speak about weight management from an honest and personal understanding of the issues... Not as a thin person who has never had a weight problem in her life!

I am a successful career woman. A trainer and facilitator, executive level leader, project manager, business owner, executive and business coach, management consultant and entrepreneur. Finally, I am a psychologist with an intense interest in people, relationships and how we choose to live our lives.

I am an open and supportive woman, lover, mother, daughter and friend. A dog owner - a veritable Dr Doolittle (it's true - they talk to me). I love to dance, enjoy yoga, crave travel and set out to experience many new things in life. I have a burning desire to continuously improve myself – not because I never feel good enough, but because I am naturally curious and thirst for knowledge. I try to live my life in honest gratitude, without judgement of others and waking each day 'full of awesome!'

A Diva is a woman is who likes who she is, is talented in her own area of expertise, knows what she wants and is not afraid to ask for it. The term originated from Latin and really means 'female deity' or Goddess. When I think of Divas, I think of Annie Lennox, Mariah Carey, Gloria Estefan, Celine Dion, Shania Twain and Aretha Franklin – amazing, talented and empowered women who know their own mind and are not afraid to be outgoing, feminine and embrace their own unique value.

I use the term 'Diva' through this book with this definition in mind… I give this to you in love and appreciation for you as a woman.

For those who have purchased this book, I have created a special 'Membership' area on my website which contains all of the resources that I refer to. Sometimes resources change and I think it's helpful to provide you with some additional information in a central area that I can easily update and keep current. Therefore, I have added some additional 'Bonuses' inside the 'Membership' area as well and will continue to provide a few little extras in there after publication.

C'mon Gorgeous… What are you waiting for?

Ms Pink
XXX

Contents

Delightful Diva

Let's start with the self...

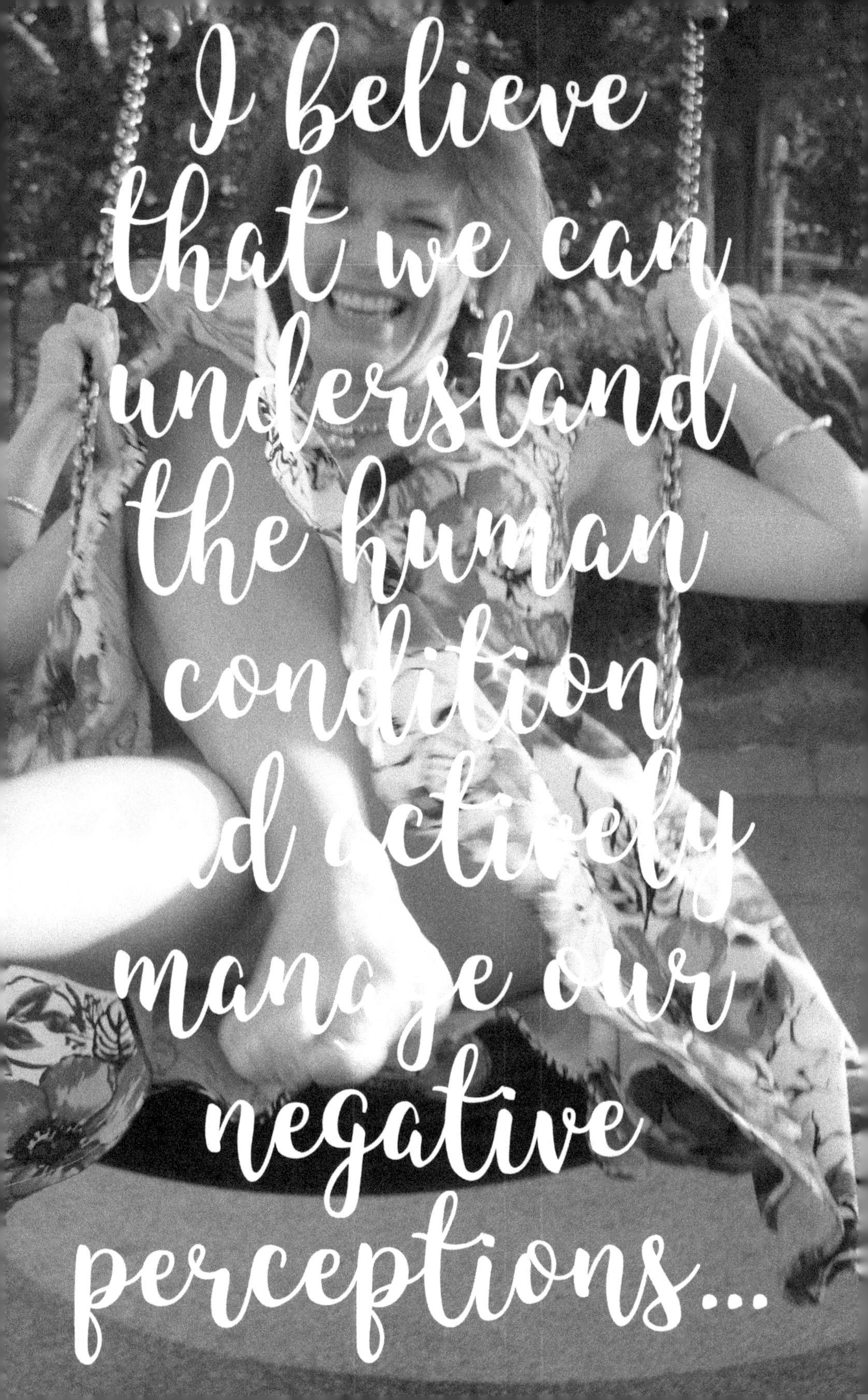

I believe that we can understand the human condition and actively manage our negative perceptions...

Chapter One

Most of us think that we know who we are, but in reality we often don't even think about it… Until we have a crisis. Then we start to question many things about ourselves.

What do I like?

What do I want out of life?

Who do I really care about?

Who wants to spend time with me?

Why would they want to spend time with me?

Who do I want to spend time with?

Who AM I? Really…

We often think of these existential questions when we're in the middle of a problem or issue that causes us to doubt ourselves. The problem is that at that point in time, we usually don't have any of the answers!

In other words, "I don't know what I like… what I want…or who I am!"

Does this sound familiar? Do you stand in front of the mirror and feel unable to gain any sense of yourself? Too often in our lives our sense of self is actually something that we gather from others. We see ourselves as we think others perceive us to be; when those people tell us we're bad we feel bad and when they tell us we're good we feel good… And if they leave our lives for any reason, we often feel lost and unsure of ourselves. This goes for our connection to family, friends and intimate relationships.

Many of us think that we ***do*** know ourselves well, that we have lives filled with purpose, and that we chose our paths in life and we are happy with that. However, when we spend some time thinking carefully about our lives we realise that in fact, what we have done is spend our lives pursuing things that others wanted for us - usually our parents or our partners. Or we have spent our lives pursuing things to prove ourselves to those same people. The other thing we do is pursue certain things to 'keep up' with our friends and acquaintances.

This is where the accumulation of material goods comes into play. We find ourselves in our leisure time shopping, believing that the accumulation of 'things' will make us feel fulfilled, justified, and valued… "Because I CAN!" But often such exercises leave you feeling even more empty. You feel riddled with guilt for spending money that you didn't really have. Sometimes the temptation of an impulse purchase is really strongly evidenced by the items hanging in your wardrobe that still have the tags attached.

Perhaps you don't lose yourself in shopping, but comfort yourself with other things, such as food. You can do this socially, connecting with others over food and a nice glass of wine. There is nothing wrong with doing this – in fact, the social interaction is wonderful for us as it gives us a sense of connection and purpose. However, I'm talking about the eating we do to make ourselves feel better - comfort for our lonely soul. Or eating because we feel a range of emotions that we can't or won't let out such as frustration, hurt, or shame.

So these are some of the things we do to compensate ourselves for how we feel. But how do we become more aware of ourselves? How can we live our lives with greater awareness, connected deeply to who we really are, what we really want and feeling fulfilled?

We need to get honest with ourselves…

Seems silly! I hear you say, "I'm honest… What is she on about?"

I'm not saying you are not an honest person. But we often live our lives in such busy-ness that we do not take the time to examine our deeper selves, our lives and determine if we are living our lives on purpose or just 'existing'!

I don't ever want to just EXIST…

That doesn't make me feel purposeful and fulfilled. We only get one life. I want to go out knowing I did the best I could for myself, my children, my parents and siblings, my partners, my friends and my community.

I'm going to get to the end of my life knowing I gave fully of myself at every waking moment. That is not necessarily an exhausting process, as I only give of myself as much as I have to give in that moment. Some days that is a lot and other days that is not much. But I do it anyway because generosity of spirit is what makes the world a more connected and fulfilled space to be.

So... How do we know about ourselves? Is it how we feel? Is it how connected we already are? We need to start with an assessment of ourselves and our lives, from where we are now.

This is probably one of the most challenging things to do for ourselves... It's a life audit. It incorporates an examination of all six areas of your life and deciding what you like, what you don't like, and finding the best strategy for yourself to move forward - with purpose.

When clients come to my office I give them the overview that I am about to share with you. I then offer them the opportunity to commit to the hard work that it will take to turn their lives around. If they are looking for someone to just 'unload' on, I tell them that isn't the kind of therapeutic work I do. I don't just do counselling or talk therapy because otherwise I find that we can talk about a situation over and over and not actually make any progress. As a result, I often say that this 'unload' space is the one your girlfriends fulfill.

When you TRULY want to change your life, you have to pick yourself up by the bootstraps and find the right type of help and commit yourself to the process. I'm not saying you have to do it alone, but you have to DO it. You can get a whole lot of support and find lots of information, but it will not change anything unless you make plans to DO something.

I want to qualify this... I'm not saying that every day you will be 100% committed to the DO. In fact, I guarantee you that there will be many days you can't. These are the opportunity points for gratitude about what you can commit yourself to and acknowledge your system's need to rest and recuperate in between. It's okay to lay down... You just need to know when to get up!

So let's get on with it...

Belief Systems

We all have a negative and a positive belief system. As human beings we are pre-programmed to focus on the negative. Think back to our evolutionary past - we needed to look out for dinosaurs and other predators. Our existence has always been dependent upon preserving life and so our system automatically protects us by scanning the environment for those things that could hurt us.

This is why it is SO difficult to maintain a positive outlook when challenging situations arise. Your brain is always scanning for danger that it becomes so focused on ensuring that you are not blind-sided that it won't allow you to focus on the positive that may be surrounding you. So trying to focus on the positive can seem absolutely impossible to do whilst focusing on the negative is super easy.

Seven Year Development Cycles

Birth to Seven

Did you know that by the time we are seven years old we ALL have the negative belief that "I am not good enough". Then we usually spend the rest of our lives trying to disprove this belief.

Why do we develop this belief?

If it doesn't come from your parents, you get it from your teachers at school. I'm not saying all adults are cruel to children, they often don't mean to be. However, human nature means that we compare ourselves to each other, our parents compare us to our siblings or cousins, and teachers compare us to our classmates. When we are constantly being compared, we are left with the feeling that we are wanting in some way.

Seven to Fourteen

Throughout school we develop ideas about ourselves like: "I'm different", "I don't belong", "I did something wrong", "I can't trust anyone", "I'm powerless", or "I'm not in control". These often develop from the interactions we have with other kids and adults - they will be stronger if you were bullied at any point.

Fourteen to Twenty-One

Enter Adolescence… That time in our lives when we disguise ourselves like chameleons to ensure that we don't stand out - because we already feel different and we are trying to combat that feeling. If you were subjected to bullying at school, you will have experienced even more difficulty during adolescence and your life experiences lead you to develop more negative self beliefs.

During adolescence, we develop an interest in our sexuality and interpersonal relationships. Depending on your sense of self at this point, you may become hyper-sexualised to try to gain acceptance, or alternatively you may avoid relationships for fear of being rejected.

It is also the time of experimentation with our own sense of self. You emerge from under the umbrella of what your parents want you to be and how they want you to behave and start to explore your own beliefs. This leads to experimentation and conflict with parents and our feelings of not being good enough are sometimes escalated to feelings of being 'bad', compounded by thoughts of being unwanted or unlovable in our negative belief system.

Twenty-One Plus

From there, depending on how your life progresses, you can develop more negative beliefs about yourself, creating a solid foundation of negativity that you spend the rest of your life as an adult trying to counter by becoming aware of your negative beliefs and developing strategies to minimise them.

By contrast, your positive sense of self doesn't get a lot of attention. Depending on your upbringing, you'll have some positive sense of self, but it is usually not very strong. When you reach adolescence, you react according to your perceived negative beliefs, and by the time you are nearing the end of high school, you decide that you can combat your negative sense of self by proving yourself to the world through your achievements either academically or through your career. So your whole sense of yourself in a positive capacity becomes focused on WHAT you do, rather than WHO you are!

You may end up in the midst of a crisis in your adult life if there is ever a situation that places pressure on what you do - like losing your job or being targeted in the work environment in some way. This is similar to what happens to women when they experience a crisis after they have children… They feel very equipped and capable in a work environment, but completely ill-prepared to cope with the responsibilities of motherhood, as babies are impossible to control.

So, when things start to go wrong in your adult life, just trying to *think positive* and get through it can feel nearly impossible.

On the following page there is an assessment called 'My Ten Things'. Please complete this now.

If you prefer, or would like additional copies, go to the website www.mspinkherself.com and find the 'Diva Resources' tab. This is a 'Membership' area specially designed for people who have purchased this book, so you will need to set up a simple profile. Here you will find a number of resources that accompany this book and I will also periodically add additional resources that may be relevant in the future.

'My Ten Things' is a list of the ten worst things that ever happened to you and the ten best things. We need to know the age you were when they happened and the belief that you had about yourself when you reflect upon that situation.

If we have been very good at externalising the negative issues in our lives, this can be a difficult exercise to do because we have always seen the issues as things that someone else did to us and we blame them. This is often the surface feeling and is not unjustified. However, underneath it all we have also blamed ourselves - even if only as a justification for **why** someone would do something negative to us.

Let me give you an example… When I was 14 I had my first serious relationship, my first real boyfriend. We went out together for three months and I thought it was true love. Then he broke up with me to go out with his best friend's sister. I was devastated but I didn't externalise the blame on him; I blamed her for stealing my boyfriend.

But internally, I was blaming myself. You see, she had a much smaller frame than I did - I wasn't really overweight, but she was smaller. I also thought she was prettier than I was. So I internalised the belief that I was not thin enough or pretty enough - therefore "I'm not wanted".

In reality, I should have blamed the boy… But I didn't. I compared myself to the new object of his affection and judged myself, then decided that I was not up to scratch and therefore his decision was justified. Interestingly, when they broke up a couple of months later, he came back to me and I rekindled that relationship. We were together for another four months until I perceived his interest was waning… So I dumped him BEFORE he could hurt me again.

This is a pattern in relationships that has stayed with me throughout my life. Each time I was reactivating the feeling that I wasn't wanted and later in life I also added "I'm not lovable enough", and that somehow "I don't deserve love".

However, these days I no longer feel like that. I have been able to resolve my underlying negative beliefs about myself and so, when a relationship ends, I am able to clearly examine my role in its demise and be okay with myself. I no longer externalise the blame, nor do I internalise it… I examine the information before me and come to terms with it, acknowledge my contribution, positive and negative, grieve the loss and move forward. I process it because to be able to move forward with my life, I have to do that.

@My Ten Things

Please complete each section below, just a couple of words to reference the event. You need to leave some space in each box in preparation for the next review process.

The ten worst things that have ever happened to me are:

	What Happened?	Age
1		
2		
3		
4		
5		
6		
7		
8		
9		
10		

The ten best things that have ever happened to me are:

	What Happened?	Age
1		
2		
3		
4		
5		
6		
7		
8		
9		
10		

Repairing the Sense of Self

You need to understand your negative belief system and make plans to resolve it. You can heal your belief systems, but sometimes you need some additional help.

Let's review…

My Beliefs

So now you have completed your 'Ten Things' list, we need to work out their underlying beliefs. As adults, we have developed adaptive strategies to combat the negative beliefs and we have good stories that we've told ourselves to support how we prefer to think about ourselves. But to get to the true beliefs, you need to switch off your brain and note where some beliefs kick you in the gut. By the same token, when you complete the good things I need you to be honest with yourself about how you REALLY feel about yourself in a positive way… Not what you would prefer to believe, but what you ACTUALLY believe.

You're a smart woman. You have learned to tell yourself all sorts of things to overcome your negative feelings. Although I know these are thoughts you don't like to give oxygen to, an honest examination of yourself really helps to clarify why you sometimes feel low or flat without explanation.

Remember what I said earlier about being honest? No one is going to see this (unless you choose to share with your sisters in our Private Facebook Group), but for your own development, you need to be true to yourself. Don't be surprised if this process makes you feel down. Be aware that it is likely to activate some feelings that we often try to avoid.

If this happens, be kind to yourself, let the feelings be acknowledged, connect with those who love and care about you and know that I am in this journey with you, and so are the other Divas. We need to understand ourselves better and a process such as this allows us to learn what needs to be addressed so we can take appropriate action to fully resolve our sense of self.

Complete the assessment of your belief systems because this will highlight if you have a high-strength or low-strength negative belief system. It is the negative beliefs that have the biggest impact on our sense of self. Once you have identified your negative and positive memories and the age you were when the situations occurred, we will be able to determine the beliefs associated with those memories.

@My Belief System

For each of the ten things on your list, give each one at least one belief. To work out what these beliefs are, we are going to utilise the 'Negative and Positive Beliefs Lists' (see **Appendix 1** and also the Diva Resources page on the website) and note ANY other belief that triggers your gut when you read it. Write the linked beliefs into the tables on the previous pages - next to the memory references.

To work out what the connected belief is, I want you to think about how each situation made you feel about yourself and list as many of the beliefs that you feel you had about yourself. This needs to be related to how you felt at the time that it happened - the first feeling you get when you think about it, the one that kicks you in the gut… We need to go with the feeling from your gut, not your head.

I want you to add the number of different negative and positive beliefs you have for each memory and note this in the 'Age' column. Next, we need to understand their strength. Again, I need you to approach this from your gut and not your head.

@Strength of our Negative Beliefs

Go to the website www.mspinkherself.com and in the 'Resources', find the document called 'Scoring Negative Belief Strength'. Complete this and note your result in your 'Revolution Roadmap' in the 'Membership' portal.

Depending on the strength of your negative belief system, the approach to finding a resolution will vary. If it is low-strength, you may be able to work through some self-development processes and see if this resolves things enough to allow you to move forward. However, what do you do if you have a high-strength negative belief system?

You will need to find yourself a good therapist. I don't want you to freak out about that idea, or denigrate it as unnecessary or a useless process because you have tried therapy before and it didn't work. I suggest you try an EMDR Therapist or a Resource State Therapist (there is a link to the various international organisations in the Member Portal or you can ask Google). The great thing about these types of therapies is that they are effective and efficient forms that actually change the underlying beliefs that you hold about yourself, and in this way you are most likely to be able resolve long-standing beliefs. You want to engage in a therapeutic process that will allow you to 'heal' the negative belief system, not just use a band-aid solution.

Let me explain…

A lot of the negative beliefs we have developed about ourselves over time have come from negative experiences that began in childhood. Up until the age of seven, and in some cases until the age of ten, we have very concrete ways of thinking. Essentially, as children we believe that good things happen when we are good, and bad things happen when we are bad. Black and White – concrete thinking, then this gets 'set'. By the age of seven, we have all developed the idea that "I am not good enough". If you didn't get that idea from your parents, you got it from school by being unfavourably compared with siblings or peers. Parents often do this between siblings, even if they are not trying to be hurtful, they often make the comparison in their impatience with our progress.

Our other life experiences then build upon this negative belief. If you are bullied or ostracised at school, you develop a sense that "I'm different - I don't belong". If you have other experiences in which you were punished harshly you feel that "I did something wrong". You may find yourself physically hurt or threatened, so you develop a sense that "I'm not safe – I'm powerless". The negative belief system is very firmly about 'who' you are.

By the time you are in your third development stage (14-21 years) you have a strong sense of your 'negative' beliefs and not much in your 'positive' beliefs to counteract them. Is it any wonder that adolescents experience very high rates of depression and anxiety? In fact, depression is the leading contributor to the burden of disease among young adults between the ages of 18-24.[1] By adulthood these rates drop significantly - partly due to the overlaying of an alternative positive belief system that is built on the basis of 'what' you do - so your success in your working life or career is crucial. We often focus on our career as the opportunity to prove ourselves and to raise our sense of self-worth in the process.

It will come as no surprise to you then to learn that many adults move forward with their lives until something threatens their work or career… Then the world seems to come crashing down on them. I liken the experience of life to having a 'toy box' in your gut - just think about a box that has a drop down lid and is easily over-filled. When bad things happen, you open the box and throw the bad thing in quickly and shut the lid. You continue to do this throughout your life with any experiences that bring with them negative self-references. You fill up the box throughout your life and, depending on your experiences, by the time you reach your mid-life your box is overflowing and you can't seem to feel good about yourself at all. Yet you can't actually put your finger on why.

No one ever told you that you had a limit to the impact of negative experience…

No one ever told you that you may be unable to just lock away all those negative beliefs…

You have been told to just think positive!

1 AIHW (2011) *Young Australians: Their Health and Wellbeing 2011* Australian Institute of Health and Welfare.

You were told to compare yourself to the poor starving children in Africa… Your life is amazing in comparison! And in truth – it is. However, within your brain, it makes no difference. You already have 'set' core negative beliefs about yourself and they were set before you were even aware of yourself. By the time you become aware, the beliefs can only be managed - you are not able to stop their activation.

From this set point, you then continue into your adult life and different negative experiences compound the negative feelings we have about ourselves and your 'box' fills up. In contrast, the positive beliefs are not very strong. They are usually focused on 'what' we do and that is easily minimised. Sometimes we become adept at building a false positive system over the top of ourselves - the front man persona - confident, outspoken, assertive. In reality, underneath is a person who does not really value themselves, they gain self-worth from seeing themselves through the eyes of those around them.

We can continue in this way for a long time… Just existing.

Our Resources

One of the other really important ways to understand our sense of self is the awareness that our personalities are made up of 'parts' and those parts are our resources. Do you have a particular behaviour or emotion that you are aware of that, when it emerges, you wish it hadn't? For example, maybe you know that there is a part of you that can get angry. You are aware that sometimes that 'angry part' reacts to things in the heat of the moment, then later you wish you hadn't responded in that way. We often respond to certain triggers and we may, or may not, be aware of what these triggers are - but we *are* aware of the feeling or behaviour that comes up and we *don't* like it.

Do you ever think "I hate it when I do (insert behaviour here)" or "I wish I didn't **feel** that way"? As children, when we have negative experiences, we develop coping skills. When we have the same experience on a regular basis, we trigger a coping mechanism and our brain grows stronger in response to that behaviour or emotion.

No one ever told you that you have a limit to the impact of negative experience...
No one ever told you that you may be unable to just 'lock away' all of those negative beliefs...
You were told to just THINK POSITIVE

That particular brain pathway becomes strong when the stimulation is repeated, which results in a physiological state of awareness that becomes a personality part[2]. I often refer to this personality part as a 'facet' of self.

We all have parts, you know them - your working part, your daughter part, your friend part, your leader, your public speaker, nurturer, mother, lover... You get the idea. These parts mostly communicate well together and share memories easily - but sometimes we are aware that we have a part that we don't like, a part that behaves in a way that we wish it didn't and this can result in inner conflict. You may be aware of times when you have 'argued with yourself' and this process is entirely normal. When all our parts are working together effectively we have balance and we are psychologically healthy.

In essence, it is our different parts that hold the different negative beliefs about ourselves. When we work with these beliefs, we are working with the part of us that holds that belief, emotion or behaviour. There are a number of ways that we can work through these negative beliefs - I mentioned EMDR Therapy earlier and if you want to work with your different parts of self, you could also contact a Resource Therapy practitioner.

How Our Beliefs Impact Our Relationships

The relationships in our adult lives often change our perception of ourselves. Perhaps friendships or intimate relationships change - we might feel rejected by those we thought we were close to or a problematic issue arises in the family, you might perceive a need to withdraw. At that time, the thing that you saw that was positive – "I'm a good partner" or "I'm a good daughter", the belief that developed because of the way you treat others (how generous and giving you are) changes.

Alternatively, the primary thing that you saw as positive, usually what you do for work, changes due to some outside influence beyond your control. All of a sudden you feel adrift, lost and afraid. As a result of these changes, your only point of self-reference is an overflowing toy box of negative belief... The positives just pale in comparison. Is it any wonder then that you feel lost?

Maybe you are reading this saying "Nope! That's not me." If so, that's wonderful! However, I think you can see how this pattern may form.

2 Emmerson, G (2014) *Resource Therapy Primer*, Old Golden Point Press, Blackwood.

Perhaps you haven't had such a high level of negative experiences in your life, in which case I'm glad that you read through this until now because if this ever happens to you in the future, you will be aware of it and know what you need to do to resolve it quickly.

Either way, I hope you understand the importance of being able to resolve the negative belief system before you can move forward. If we don't, we drag it like a ball and chain throughout our life when we don't need to!

Sense of Self

When you have a much better sense of self, you can look in the mirror and be clear about who you are and what value you bring to the world. You can greet each day with gratitude and wake up full of 'awesome'. You can be kind to yourself when bad things happen and you feel the need to lay down a lot, to curl up in the foetal position on the couch and drink copious amounts of wine.

It happens!

When you have full acceptance of yourself, you can accept that it is a temporary state, a moment in time when you need to acknowledge the impact of negative forces around you, without beating yourself up about the fact that you need time to process, to work through things. We need to be honest with ourselves at this point and acknowledge our part in any negative outcome. We need to do this without judgement, from a place of self-empathy and kindness.

@Self-Worth Inventory

On the following page there is an assessment called the 'Self Worth Inventory'. Please complete this now. If you prefer, there is an online assessment that you can do on the website in the 'Resources' area.

Complete this and score it using the scoring information also in the 'Resources' area. Note your result in your 'Revolution Roadmap' in the 'Membership' portal.

Answer each question as honestly as you can, using the following key:

1 - Definitely not or almost never *2 - Probably not or seldom*
3 - Probably yes or often *4 - Definitely yes or almost always*

1	I am truly content with the way I look	
2	I can accomplish almost any task I attempt	
3	I consider my ability to think and reason adequate	
4	I think people enjoy being with me	
5	I am satisfied with the degree of success I am experiencing so far in my life	
6	I feel as worthwhile when I'm just having a good time as when I'm doing something constructive	
7	I consistently forgive myself when I blow it	
8	When I make a mistake I can stop myself from thinking negative things; such as I'm stupid, can't do anything right, etc	
9	I can honestly say that I love myself	
10	Deep down I feel that I am likeable just the way I am	
11	When I look at myself in the mirror I am happy with what I see	
12	I feel competent to take on most any job or challenge I face	
13	I am genuinely happy with the level of my intelligence	
14	I feel good about my personality	
15	Overall, I regard myself as successful in life	
16	I feel valuable and worthwhile as a person, even when I fail	
17	When I do something wrong or unwise, I quickly get over being angry with myself	
18	My thoughts toward myself are usually positive, rather than negative or critical	
19	Even though I am not perfect, I appreciate and love myself	
20	Though I realise I am not perfect, deep down I truly feel that I am a good person	
	Total Score	

Explanation and Scoring Self-Worth Inventory

This inventory attempts to measure ten areas of self-worth. To determine your score in each area, add your scores as shown below. For example, if your score was 2 for question #1 and 3 for question #11, then your total score for the area of Appearance would be 5.

Total Score for Each Area

1	*Appearance - Q1 & Q11*	
2	*Competence - Q2 & Q12*	
3	*Intelligence - Q3 & Q13*	
4	*Personality - Q4 & Q14*	
5	*Success - Q5 & Q15*	
6	*Unconditional Worth - Q6 & Q16*	
7	*Self-Forgiveness - Q7 & Q17*	
8	*Acceptance of Weakness - Q8 & Q18*	
9	*Self-Love - Q9 & Q19*	
10	*Freedom from Guilt - Q10 & Q20*	

If your total score was two or below for any areas, you may want to concentrate on improving your self-worth in those areas. Now look at your overall score. Compare your score with the comments below.

Total Score Comment

76-80 - If you scored in this range, you appear to have excellent self-worth. Possibly you see yourself more highly than you ought.

66-75 - You seem to have a healthy view of yourself and should have few issues with self-worth, unless you scored very low in specific areas.

56-65 - Overall, you appear to be neither high nor low in self-worth, but there may be specific areas which need attention.

46-55 - There is considerable room for growth in your self-worth, or you might be experiencing some low-mood at present.

0-45 - You have a challenging journey ahead. You need to be congratulated for taking the first step by working through this book.

A score **below 35** may indicate a level of depression. It is important that you consult your doctor or therapist about this result.

Note: No test can adequately describe the self-worth of everyone. A score below 50 is not a failure, but you may want to discuss it with a therapist

Knowing Ourselves

Once we are able to resolve our sense of self, we are able to more easily live in the moment. We can be mindful – not reliving the past nor fearing the future. It is very difficult to live mindfully or focus on the positive if we haven't resolved our negative belief system. However, once we know ourselves, there is no limit to our capabilities.

If you haven't already (or it has been a long time) I want you to watch the movie 'Runaway Bride' with Julia Roberts and Richard Gere. The main 'takeaway' I want you to note in this movie is how in each of the four relationships that Maggie (Julia Roberts) has, her tastes change, from the way she eats her eggs to her favourite leisure activities; she moulds herself to be what she believes her intimate partner wants her to be – just like him! This is what I like to call a 'Chameleon Complex' and it develops from not having a good sense of self.

Adolescence is the time when we develop who we really want to be. We do this in contrast to our parents, which is why we often rebel against their view of who they think we should be. We try to be like our friends – to fit in and not be different. It is towards the end of this developmental stage (18-21) that we get more comfortable with who WE are - our likes and dislikes - and how we choose to present ourselves to the world.

But some of us never get to that point – we stay in that chameleon space, changing and moulding ourselves as we go through life to ensure that we fit in with each group we come into contact with. When this happens we find ourselves in our mid-life not knowing who we really are and what we actually want for ourselves.

This seems to be particularly true for women. We often commit ourselves to relationships and families and develop our sense of who we are because of our roles in life – daughter, sister, wife, and mother. Perhaps you have come to this book because you have not been able to fulfil the role of wife and mother - and this leaves you feeling lost about your sense of purpose in life.

This is why we need to be clear about what we really believe about ourselves as human beings, and as women. We need to be able to stand in front of the mirror and really **see** ourselves for WHO we are - not what we look like. We need to actually like what we see…

My Opportunity to Repair

I was 28 years old when the opportunity to begin to repair my negative belief system really presented itself to me, in the form of a bus. Long story short, I had an accident - I was hit by a bus as a pedestrian and lived to tell the tale. Surprisingly, I only suffered minor injuries but the trauma took its toll on my mental health. I suffered Post Traumatic Stress Disorder (PTSD) and secondary Depression.

At that time in my life I had two children aged two and four, and a husband who was neither understanding nor supportive. I spent a full year in therapy and I took antidepressant medication for nine months of that. I have often told people that the bus saved my life! You see, I was a very good repressor. I had never dealt with the emotional issues of my childhood and I was a big believer in the need to just *soldier on*. In fact, prior to my accident, I had a friend who had suffered from depression and I admit that I just didn't get it. I tried to be supportive, but I honestly didn't understand why she just didn't pick herself up by the bootstraps and 'get on with it'!

Due to the nature of my accident, I blamed myself and I felt responsible. This is the breeding ground for PTSD, but what is interesting about my specific case is that the linkages to all of the other negative beliefs that I had about myself were suddenly all out there and raw. Remember my analogy of the toy box? In this case, it was as if the bus smashed my toy box to pieces and all of the toys (my negative experiences) that I had neatly packed away in there were suddenly strewn across the road and I couldn't get them back together. It was impossible for me to fix it and I really just dropped my bundle at that point.

I had some physical injuries, so I saw the doctor. But it was about a month before I went back to the doctor and told him the full extent of my issues. I was having regular panic attacks, I was lethargic, yet unable to sleep effectively. I couldn't think straight and I was struggling to take care of myself and my children. I had taken to not getting dressed at all during the day and this was so unlike me that I knew there was something wrong.

The doctor referred me to a psychologist and we discussed medication, but I thought medication was for weak people. I was prepared to go and talk about it and I thought that would sort it out and I could just pull myself out of this. After all, nothing had been able to get me down before!

I found a psychologist, and thankfully she had trained in EMDR Therapy. This is a big part of the reason why I later became an EMDR therapist, because I knew from personal experience that it really works! In my experience, EMDR Therapy isn't just a band-aid solution, helping to repress things again - it really heals.

However, within a couple of months, even though I was seeing the therapist, I was still really struggling and the issues that had come up for me as a result of my accident went right back to my childhood. I was working through these things but my system was still really struggling.

I recall the day when I realised I needed to do more. I had experienced a very restless night, during which I had decided that I just needed to kill myself; that everyone would be better off without me as I was just a useless burden. I HONESTLY believed that! My children were two and four years old and my husband was an alcoholic, but somewhere in my brain I believed that they would all be better off without me.

Thankfully, within the haze of confusion and despair, there was a very small voice that was whispering to me that I really needed to get some help! And I did.

I went back to the doctor and he prescribed antidepressant medication. It took several weeks to start working effectively, but I was aware that I was then able to function a little better, certainly not like the old me, but I was able to manage day-to-day and I could think a little more clearly. I didn't like the side effects from the medication, but taking it allowed my system to work, and this allowed me to function enough to fully engage with my therapy and work through my issues.

Once my therapeutic work was complete, I was able to ease myself off the antidepressants and I have never looked back. It's not to say that I haven't had other periods in my life where I have been low, but because I had resolved my underlying negative belief system, those low periods have never taken hold like that again. I now approach my low points (and we all have them as it is a normal part of the human existence) in full awareness and I am able to work through my issues.

That was the one thing about the whole bus incident that I really didn't like... I used to be able to repress things really easily. Something bad would happen and I would just suck it down into the pit of my gut and put the emotional lid on it. Since my accident, I can no longer do that.

My Thoughts

When I experience difficult things in my life now, I have to take the time to process through them as they are happening. This is much healthier for my psyche, but sometimes I get annoyed with it because the process takes time. This is why I say we need to deal with the issues from our past and clear out our negative beliefs.

@Character Strengths

To help round out our understanding of ourselves, I would like you to have a look at your character strengths. Character strengths are the positive parts of your personality that impact how you think, feel and behave and are important keys to understanding how you can be your best self.

Developed by some amazing pioneers in the field of 'Positive Psychology', this information comes from the VIA Survey, which is regarded as a central tool of positive psychology.[3] There are 24 character strengths and they are categorised into six different virtues – wisdom, courage, humanity, justice, temperance and transcendence.

Wisdom – cognitive strengths that involve the acquisition and use of knowledge. This area includes creativity, curiosity, judgement, love of learning and perspective.

Courage – emotional strengths that show the ability to accomplish things in the face of opposition, either from others (external) or from within (internal). This area includes bravery, perseverance, honesty and zest.

Humanity – interpersonal strengths that involve connecting and caring for others. This area includes love, kindness and social intelligence.

Justice – civic strengths that underlie healthy community life. This area includes teamwork, fairness and leadership.

Temperance – strengths that protect us against excess. These include forgiveness, humility and self-regulation.

Transcendence – strengths that forge connections to the larger universe and provide meaning. These include hope, humour, spirituality, gratitude and appreciation of beauty and excellence.

Character strengths are different to your other strengths, such as your unique skills, talents, interests and resources, because these are the components that reflect the *real* you - who you are at your core. Every one of us possesses each of the 24 character strengths in different degrees, giving

3 https://www.viacharacter.org/www/Character-Strengths/Science-Of-Character

each person a unique character profile. We are going to discover your personal character strengths profile by completing the online assessment.

Please go to the 'Resources' area and click on the link for 'Character Strengths' – this is a free online survey tool that produces a report of your character strengths in rank order. You will receive a downloadable report of your strengths and you can choose if you would like share that information with me or not. If you would like to take advantage of my **Extra Special BONUS** at the end of this book, it can be useful to share this with me. However, it is just as easy for you to download your report and you could share it with me later if you choose to.

Looking to the Future

Once we have cleared the issues from our past, understood what has held us back and prevented us getting what we want for ourselves in our lives, we then need to look to our future and work out what we want from it and have a soft plan for getting there. I often talk about that plan as a hand-drawn life map on a crinkled up piece of paper, and you hold a pen in your hand so that you can draw in a new path at any point in the future.

Then we need to live in the moment, approach the everyday in mindfulness…

Mindfulness is a concept we explore more in Chapter Six – Dharma Diva. Resolution of the negative belief system allows us to move more of 'who' you are into the positive belief system.

I am a good person - generous and valued
I am loveable
I can trust people
I can accept that some things are out of my control
I can be assertive about what I want or need
I can stand up for myself
I can make mistakes and often do
I deserve good things - to love and be loved

I am allowed to be kind to myself
I will nurture myself without guilt
I can take care of my health and my body
I can live in the moment - in awareness of my goals and a loose map of how I'm going to get there...

I am Delightful!

When experience is viewed in a certain way, it presents nothing but doorways into the soul

Jon Kabat-Zinn

Delectable Diva

So – the relationship has ended…

I believe that we deserve to be loved, connected and embraced...

We can be both

Chapter Two

Many people believe that because divorce is so common in our modern society that it is no longer a big deal. Wrong.

It has a huge impact on your sense of yourself as a person – the perception of rejection that comes from feeling unwanted, or feeling that the other person does not love you enough to fix it. Depending on your sense of self, you may have decided that you were badly hurt, your trust is broken and you will never allow yourself the opportunity to have another relationship again.

Alternatively, you may be feeling that you do not have to spend the rest of your life alone, but the idea of opening yourself up again and making yourself vulnerable feels too painful. However, when the isolation and sense of loneliness kicks in, the fear that you'll be alone forever can be overwhelming.

The Western Marriage

We believe that love is a precondition for marriage, but this assumption is not shared in cultures that practise arranged marriages. In fact, in most western societies, marital choices, especially those by women, were strongly influenced by considerations of economic security, family background and professional status or educational equality. Cultures vary in the importance they place on romantic love.

There is an argument that says that the reason that divorce rates are so much higher in western societies is because we do place so much emphasis on love and emotional support. Other cultures do this very differently. Yes, there are other considerations including choice and oppression that impact marriage in other cultures, and this will impact divorce rates. However, the main point I want you to take from this is that in western societies, expectations of relationships have significantly changed over time due to the changing nature of women's roles in our society. In essence, we now have more choice around our lives and how we live them.

Why Do Relationships End?

There are multiple reasons that couples separate - but essentially one or both of them are unhappy and they have moved into a pattern of 'relating' that is stuck and immoveable. Potentially only one of the partners wants to resolve the issues. Often one of you has left the relationship emotionally long before the physical separation.

We get stuck in patterns of relating to each other that repeat the same problems over and over... We need to take a leaf from Einstein - only an insane person repeats the same mistake over and over, expecting a different result. Eventually, one member of the partnership realises this and if the other partner is not interested in resolving the problem, they separate or devolve into a 'parallel' relationship.

The only way to resolve this is firstly to be aware of the issues and their triggers. Then you need to have two people committed to resolve the issues and address the triggers. Without 100% commitment from both parties, the relationship is unable to remain a connected one.

There are a number of issues that can arise in a relationship including:

- Financial
- Emotional
- Parenting style
- Household tasks and responsibilities
- Extended family
- Communication style
- Sexual incompatibility (changing needs)

Modern society tells us that it's easier to just walk away and find someone else, or stay single, than it is to deal with the issues in the relationship. This is especially true if you have had these issues for several years. To correct the issues in a relationship you have to work really hard at it, but sometimes you just find that you don't have the energy left to do it, or you are the only one who wants to do it.

Infidelity

No matter which way we like to think about it, or how much mud we want to sling at the other party, the reason for infidelity is usually because the person who was unfaithful was unhappy in the relationship and sought solace in another connection.

There are certain people and personality types who, although they often appear to be very strong personalities and seem very sure of themselves, have a very low sense of self. These people often engage in *serial cheating* whilst they are supposed to be in a committed relationship - it's about proving themselves and boosting their own egos, but on the whole, this is not the norm.

Many people who are in unhappy relationships will find themselves drawn to an alternative person in their life, usually through work or some other social connection. If the opportunity comes up for a connection with that person, they can become so caught up in the romantic possibilities around that connection that they jump in. There is often regret afterwards, sometimes coupled with guilt and shame. Depending on what is happening in the committed relationship, the act of infidelity can be a wake-up call for the person to take action to resolve the differences in the committed relationship, or a prompt that they should leave.

Even if they decide that they want to leave, there are often other contributing factors to their decision-making which can result in a feeling that they can't leave - these can be for financial, emotional or some other reasons. As a result, some people choose, instead, to become involved in an extended affair.

Alternatively, the person who cheated may decide that the committed relationship needs to be fixed. They may choose to hide or disclose their infidelity, which will result in a change around how they approach their spouse. If they hide it, they can be wracked with guilt and start trying to overcompensate in their relationship. They may resolve the issues of their own accord, but usually the guilt will take its toll at some point and the relationship will eventually end. If they disclose it - they run the risk that their partner will reject them, despite them stating that they want to fix the relationship.

I am often asked if a relationship can recover from infidelity. I believe that it can, but it requires absolute honesty from both parties, an enormous commitment to the healing process and a willingness on the part of the 'cheater' to live their life completely open to their partner to allow the re-establishment of trust.

In essence, a relationship will breakdown due to an erosion of trust. If not through infidelity, through a belief that your partner doesn't love or support you enough to fix an issue. Alternatively viewed, you don't trust them to 'fix it'.

Just as I highlighted above around infidelity, a relationship can recover from ANY issue if there is absolute honesty and a commitment to the healing process from both parties. So we need to understand ourselves in that process - what we can control and what we cannot, recognise our own contribution to the breakdown and work our way forward.

So – what do you know about yourself?

@ Review of Behaviours

Go to the website and in the 'Resources', find the document called 'Review of Behaviours'. Complete this and note your result in your 'Revolution Roadmap'.

It is important to note that I am expecting that for most relationship dimensions, your relationship will have scored less than 15, and most likely less than 10 – otherwise you would not be reading this book as your relationship would still be thriving (unless something else went drastically wrong). The reason why I ask you to evaluate your previous relationship is because we need to understand ourselves, and what happens when resentment builds in our relationships. This is so that we can learn from this rather than repeat the same mistakes again in our future relationships.

My Behaviour in Relationships

Answer the questions in each dimension according to this guide:

Never – 0 Rarely – 1 Sometimes – 2 Often – 3 Regularly – 4

My Thoughts

Who's to Blame?

Often when we are unhappy (and we don't have a good sense of self) we will seek to blame others for issues and never want to look at our own behaviour and how it may have contributed to the problem: this is called 'externalising'.

One of the classic examples I use to explain this concept is those moments when you are out with a friend or partner and see a woman in the shopping centre and you judge her based on her appearance. The reason we do this is because there is something about the other woman that has made you feel insecure or unsure of your own value. Before you know it you are saying to your companion, "Will you look at her! My goodness, fancy being seen out in public looking like that!"

This is a perfect example of how we use others to try to elevate ourselves in our own esteem. In making an initial judgement of the other, you found something about them to be potentially positive and at a subconscious level felt something negative about yourself. As a result, you sought to bring her down a peg or two in your esteem, to allow yourself to rise above her and therefore feel better about yourself. We use judgement to do this and it is very destructive.

When I am sitting having coffee with someone who engages in this type of behaviour, I will often gently ask "What is it about her that suddenly made you feel bad about yourself?" It is imperative that we understand that this type of externalising behaviour is often how we have learned to cope with the feelings of inadequacy that we feel about ourselves. However, it is not helpful and does not lead to any long-term improvement in your self-esteem.

The alternative is internalising, and this can be equally destructive, but in a different way. If we internalise in the same scenario, when you see someone in the shopping centre and you admire her appearance, there may be something about the other woman that has made you feel insecure or unsure of your own value. You will usually say nothing but start the negative internal dialogue about how 'she looks so much better than you do' and that 'you will never be able to look that good'. You do the same thing as above, but the negative dialogue is never put 'out there' - rather it is used as a berating internal voice. Before you know it, you suddenly feel like ordering a large piece of cheesecake and you withdraw from any conversation around you because you instantly feel like you don't have anything of great value to contribute.

The process is essentially the same - we have compared ourselves to another person, judged and found ourselves wanting. *How* we verbalise or validate that judgement is the only real difference here. Where we need to get to is a place where we are secure enough in **who** we are, that we can watch the world go by and observe it without judgement. When we are able to do this, we are truly accepting of ourselves.

Relationship Review... What went wrong?

One of the things that we avoid doing when a relationship ends is to step back and take a good hard look at what went wrong and how we contributed to the breakdown of the relationship. Many of you will do a double take on the last sentence. Yes – I am asking you to be honest with yourself and understand what *you* did that contributed to the breakdown of the relationship. This is absolutely critical if you want to be able to process the loss and move forward.

Depending on how many relationships you have had (you only need to have two longish ones to see this), you will likely be aware of some similarities in how your partner treated you. It is this phenomenon that allows us to almost duplicate the same type of relationship over and over. Each relationship has its own dynamic energy, and I adapted a categorisation system based on Imago Therapy and how I see people behaving in their relationships.

In my experience most relationships have a 'self nurturer' who I refer to as a '1' and an 'other nurturer' who I refer to as a '2'. 1s usually put themselves first and 2s tend to put the other person's needs ahead of their own. You can have two people in a relationship who are the same, but it is often the case that we pair up with a partner who works differently to us.

In a relationship, I am very definitely a 2 - this means that I give a lot of myself to the relationship. I sacrifice my own needs and desires for the benefit of the other person, so I am often attracted to a 1. In a relationship, a 1 will often be the person who 'withdraws' when they are not happy. The 2 is the person who will pursue the 1 and ask 'What's wrong? Is everything okay?' They are often 'in their face' to try to engage the other and reconnect.

As the 1 withdraws, the 2 pursues and tries to draw out the issues to regain a connection. Over time, the 2 gets burned out from always being the pursuer and eventually the 2 will stop actively chasing the 1 and withdraw from the relationship altogether - often to the 'surprise' of the 1.

You can have an effective relationship with two 1s or two 2s in a relationship, as 1s will take care of their own needs first, so they each look after themselves and often both feel okay in that. Two 2s will constantly give to the other, but they are always getting back from their partner in return – so this also creates 'balance' in the relationship.

However, we often find that in relationships you have a 1 and a 2, a taker and a giver, and this often results in an imbalance over time and ultimately sees the demise of the relationship. You often hear about how the 'nice guys' always end up with really horrible girls and the 'lovely' girls always end up with the self-absorbed guys… Perhaps this is why.

It may surprise you to learn that we set a blueprint for our ideal partner by the time we are seven years old and it is based primarily on the negative traits of our primary caregivers - usually our parents. This process is outlined more thoroughly in the groundbreaking book 'Getting the Love you Want' by Dr Harville Hendrix (1988), this book provides the foundations of Imago Therapy.

Understanding how we got into the relationship is important, and we examine this in more detail later. You really need to understand this phenomenon and how it impacts your subconscious decision-making around partners before you can move forward, hopefully not repeating the same pattern.

However, what is important to acknowledge at this point is that, regardless of how the relationship ended, you also did things that contributed to it ending. You may feel that everything is your partner's fault, but ultimately we also feed into the demise of the relationship in some way.

My Marriage Failure

When I first started having issues in my marriage and we separated for the first time (we tried to reconcile five times before I finally gave up!), I was firmly of the belief that the primary issue was my husband's problem and I was not going to tolerate it anymore. Through our reconciliation and re-separation processes over the following six years, I became more aware of how I impacted upon the breakdown of the relationship.

Inner Peace begins
the moment you
choose not to
allow another
person or event
to control your
emotions

Pema Chodron

When we first separated, I was still trying to take control of the situation and I gave him an ultimatum. We separated, but then he capitulated on my ultimatum and we tried again. However, as I'm sure you can guess, eventually the old behaviour started to creep back in and he blamed me for making him comply with my ultimatum. In complying, he had made a decision to change his behaviour that he was never really interested in changing, and in changing it he began to resent me for forcing the change - so we tried to compromise and start again. This pattern continued for several years, each one beginning with me giving him an ultimatum, him capitulating and being compliant for a while, but eventually resenting me for forcing him to do something he didn't want to do!

For my part, I had to grow to a point where I could admit that I was the one who had made the mistake of marrying him in the first place. You see - I was young, only 21 years old and I married him believing I could change him! This was my first big mistake in this relationship.

What's interesting is that many years later a Jyotish (a Vedic astrologer) picked out this period of time in my life, a seven-year period that started from our first separation and ended with our divorce, as the major karmic learning period for my life. Do you know what my major karmic learning for this life was?

You CANNOT change another human being… And you SHOULD NOT want to!

In my youth, I had the arrogance to believe that although he was a good man, he would become better when he did what I wanted him to do. As an older woman I can now look back and laugh at myself… The control I sought to have and the belief that somehow I had the right to make demands of another person to become the person that I wanted him to be, rather than who he really was. It was quite ludicrous really.

Many of us seek to control our partners, get them to do things that we want them to do, rather than letting them be themselves. Whether it is the way they look or how they dress, their career or financial position, their friends and their social activities or their eating or drinking habits, many of us try to change our partners in varying ways - some of them not very subtle!

So in my initial attempts to control the relationship issues, I still tried to 'control' my husband's behaviour by forcing compliance with my decision which, post-reconciliation, he would always rebel against. As time progressed and I repeated the same ultimatum, and we repeated the same pattern (albeit over varying lengths of time) I subtly changed my position. I stopped making ultimatums and I started to resent him. I got to the point where I had real difficulty even being nice to him. It was around this time that I found myself attracted to someone else - this had never happened before, and I knew that it marked a significant shift in my own mind.

In the end, I ended the relationship shouldering the blame on myself. I never cheated, as it was not in my nature to do so. However, I knew that the fact that I was contemplating an alternative interaction in my mind meant that the relationship I was in was making me very unhappy and I had to get out of it! My approach to ending it the last time was also very different, and it was very difficult to get my husband to accept my decision, because:

I didn't give him an ultimatum,

I didn't blame him,

I hadn't done anything deliberately to hurt him…

I just told him I was done, over it and I wanted a divorce. No more opportunities to 'fix' anything. It was quite obvious to me that we wanted to live our lives in different ways and I was no longer going to blame him for him wanting it to be different to mine. I took the blame for marrying him in the first place, knowing that I wanted to change him. I apologised to him for that, but I was no longer going to try and force us to be on the same page when we really hadn't been for 13 years. We had tried, but we had to acknowledge that we couldn't fix it because it had really never been a single thing that was broken.

We had always had two very different perspectives and they could never be reconciled.

It was more painful for him at this point. It is usually women who choose to leave a relationship and the men are often left wondering why when in truth they miss many of the subtle clues that women leave them and they don't really listen to what a woman is telling them about how she feels. Often when women talk emotion men hear a problem that they need to fix, but they usually don't validate her feelings, and this is often the cause of disagreement and creates challenges in intimate relationships.

In the end, we were able to part in a reasonably amicable way, mainly because we had tried many times to sort it out and as a result of my increasing self- awareness, I was completely honest about my own involvement in the development of the problem and I wasn't just blaming him. In fact, I tried to take the blame completely on myself because I also did not want to leave any room for his male brain to think that he could fix it! After all that was why we had spent six years trying to resolve *unresolvable* issues.

So, you're out… There is no going back

Take time to understand yourself and your contribution to the breakdown of the relationship. It is absolutely critical that you have clarity around this so that you can move forward. I'm not talking about rushing headlong into another relationship, but you want to ensure that you are not still hanging onto things that will prevent you getting on with your life.

You have clarity…

You are resourceful…

You are Gorgeous!

Ready for a new relationship?

Perhaps you have recently ended a relationship and would like to reconnect with an intimate partner again. Or, you may not have had an intimate partner for an extensive period of time and this may be for a host of reasons. If you are contemplating a new intimate relationship (or pretending that it doesn't matter that you don't have one), I want you to answer this one question.

Why do you want to be in a relationship?

If the answer is because you are lonely – then you have come to the right place. Not because I'm going to tell you it's okay to want a relationship for that reason - it's not. However, it means that I can show you how you can first become more accepting of yourself and your own needs and desires BEFORE you enter into your next relationship. If you do this, the next relationship will be much more like the kind of relationship you have always wanted for yourself.

You CANNOT change another human being... And you SHOULD NOT want to!

If you want to be in a relationship because you believe it is one of those things that would enhance the life that you already live and love - then you can probably stop reading. Although it wouldn't hurt you to take a little time to review the information here and decide for yourself if you are *truly* ready.

Women and Desire

Firstly, let's just highlight the fact that we all want to be desired - we often confuse this with being wanted or even worse, needed! Our own sense of ourselves as women is often buoyed by the sense that we can give to others. It is the natural nurturing way of women - we are born nurturers. So we often give of ourselves… So much so, that we can lose ourselves in the process.

This is a symptom of co-dependency. Now before you get 'freaked out' over that word (the psychological profession are forever telling us it's a bad thing), I need you to hear this… ALL women have a tendency to be a little co-dependent, and if you are NOT, it is usually because you once were and you were hurt in the process, so you made an active decision to hold yourself back from giving so much of yourself in the future - as a protection mechanism.

Biologically we are pre-programmed to nurture - to give of ourselves to partners, family, friends, children and anyone else who comes along. This is the essence of being feminine. I'm not being disrespectful, or in any way anti-feminist. Allow me expand a little about why we do this and why it is something we need to understand about ourselves and EMBRACE it!

Our biological roots are at the core of this. We are destined to give life in our bodies - that is how we were designed. Regardless of whether or not our bodies ever actually produce life, the emotions associated with the need to nurture and care are already there, in our DNA. Without this, the survival of the human race would have been in jeopardy. We can't just reject it, or claim that the males in the species don't have as much drive to nurture. We need to understand that we are all individuals and we are all born with varying abilities to nurture and care - but the difference in how this manifests is often very different between men and women. That's a good thing!

I just want you to understand that to nurture and care are part of your biological make-up as women. So, understand yourself and accept that this is how life is. The centre of a woman's nature is her heart and there is good reason for that. But modern society has taught us that our heart cannot be followed or trusted, as it is also the seat of pain!

However, you need to get out of your head and more into your heart, but we need to do it with a little balance. For this to work most effectively, we need to rely on our 'intuition' - and this is something that we are taught as women in modern western societies NOT to trust. Yet, if you reflect back on the relationships that have gone wrong, you will usually find that your intuition was telling you that there was something wrong - through your heart - and your head overruled it because it was looking for hard, concrete evidence! Proof before you were able to act... But in the end, your intuition was right all along.

@Clarifying Our Needs

In the 'Resources' area on the website, locate a document called 'Clarifying Our Needs'. Complete this and note your result in your 'Revolution Roadmap' in the 'Membership' portal.

Complete this using the 'Traits List' (see **Appendix 2**) and follow the instructions in the 'Revolution Roadmap', which is where you should note your result. It is important that you spend some time in reflection about this information as you read through the rest of this chapter.

The Blueprint

A little known fact is that we set the blueprint for who we seek as a life partner by the time we are seven years old. This blueprint is based on our primary caregivers and can be an amalgamation of both our parents (if they were both around) or based on the person who took primary care of you.[4] What's really interesting is that this blueprint is based on their NEGATIVE traits.

Yes... Really!

As human beings we are very complex creatures. We seek in our life partner the same negative traits as our primary caregivers because we are trying to prove that the problem is the caregiver, not us!

4 https://www.amazon.com/Getting-Love-You-Want-Anniversary/dp/0805087001

Let me give you a scenario…

My mother was not very affectionate and she rarely told us that she loved us. As a child I used to throw myself on her and seek cuddles and comfort, ask to have my back rubbed and a range of other requests for physical touch. These were often unmet, despite my requests. This was my mother's issue - but as a child I came to believe she didn't give me physical affection because she didn't care enough about me.

So, as an adult I am consciously seeking a partner who is physically affectionate, but subconsciously seeking a partner who is not! You see, my subconscious has decided that if I can get the person who is not usually affectionate to give me affection, then I can prove the issue is with my mother and not because I am not worthy of affection.

Inevitably, I believe I choose someone who is physically affectionate, but usually after the 'Honeymoon Period' (the first 12-18 months in a relationship) the physical affection drops away and I start to feel that I am no longer loved and that I am the problem - I don't deserve to be given the affection that I so desire to make me feel loved.

As you can see, this becomes an enormous problem because I am completely unaware that this is what I need in my relationship and I have certainly never expressed that need to my partner. But I become unhappy, I start finding fault in the relationship and things begin to deteriorate until ultimately I walk away from the relationship and eventually go seeking another relationship that will fill the void I have within me for physical affection.

In this way, I set in motion the 'repeating' pattern of behaviour that reinforces my negative belief about myself - that I do not deserve love and affection.

Do you think that my mother could have ever known how her natural way of being would affect me?

Do you think that any of my partners would have understood how their behaviour reinforced this negative belief I held about myself?

Do you think that I had any idea of what I was really looking for in my relationships and why I repeated the SAME pattern over and over and just felt worse and even more rejected in the process?

These days I understand myself and my own needs much better. I always recommend to couples who come to me for therapy to first undertake an examination of their 'Love Languages' - to see how compatible they are.

@5LoveLanguages.com

I want you to go to the website above and complete the assessment of your 'Love Languages' for yourself. Take a bit of time reviewing the information from Gary Chapman, as it really helps to understand ourselves and what our own love languages are. This provides a really valuable resource for any relationship. Complete this and note your result in your 'Revolution Roadmap'.

Gary breaks down our love languages into five areas - physical touch, acts of service, gifts, quality time and words of affirmation. I would ask you to complete the assessment of your love languages based on your situation now - you can take it as a single person. It will list your love languages in order. It is the top two that are the most significant.

You see we all have different actions and behaviours that we use to communicate love. If yours are different to your partner's, you will feel disconnected and like things aren't working. If your love languages match, you will often overlook other issues in the relationship because the connection feels VERY strong. You need to understand yourself and you need to understand any potential partner that comes along. It is not that you CANNOT make it work if you speak different love languages - you can, but it will take more active effort on both your parts.

It is useful to have any new partner also undertake this assessment as it will help to make you aware from the outset if your love languages are actually different, so that you can adjust and make allowances for each other. In the beginning of a new relationship, we utilise all five love languages, but usually revert to our primary two after the honeymoon period is over.

My number one is physical touch, closely followed by quality time. This explains why, as a child, I actively sought physical touch from my parents. It also explains why I have stayed in relationships that were not good for me, but in which the physical touch and quality time components were there. I am now aware of the link and I always ask any potential partners to complete the assessment for themselves so that I can have a good understanding of what is important for them and I can share with them what is important for me.

If they also match me on my top two - even if they were in the opposite order, the connection will feel positive. However, my bottom two are words of affirmation and gifts. If they were their top two, then in the long term we are going to experience challenges in the relationship and would need to make a more concerted effort to meet the needs of the other.

You see, we show our partners that we love them in the way we want to be shown love. So, I will touch a partner and I will make space in my life to ensure that I spend a lot of time with them. Alternatively, if I have a partner with opposing love languages then they may not make themselves available to me. Instead, they will buy me gifts and send me messages telling me that they care but I will not FEEL that care, concern or love from them. If I am unaware of this difference, I will become despondent and feel that my partner does not want to spend time with me because they don't care… Yet that isn't necessarily the case.

So you can see, if we speak different love languages, we set ourselves up to feel that the relationship lacks fulfilment (due to our unmet needs and the perception of why they are unmet), yet most of it is in our own minds.

It becomes just another nail in the coffin… But one often used to justify the negative beliefs we hold about ourselves, despite the fact that these are often not something we are consciously aware of. You should be more aware of your negative beliefs now from Chapter One, which is the chapter on Self, but to date you have carried these with you and utilised varying relationships to justify these negative beliefs.

Sense of Self

This notion is extremely important in explaining why you attract the relationships that you do. If you have had multiple relationships, you may find a common thread among them. This may be very obvious, like you choose partners who are emotionally unavailable, or perhaps for you it is a little less obvious. However, if you take the time to review them, on closer examination of your relationships, you will discover that they all made you feel the same negative belief about yourself.

So why does it happen? Surely we learn from our mistakes?

Unless we reach awareness of our own issues, we will continue to repeat the same mistakes over and over again. It is like the universe is

trying to teach you something, but you have to be open to listening. I am the first to admit that I have gone from a relationship that was a *heart* decision and run headlong into a *head* decision, believing that I had chosen differently and that would make it better. Invariably, however, the head decision looks different on the surface, but the underlying issues remain the same. The other factor here is TIME.

Two Years

From my experience, I recommend that you should *not* make a commitment to another person in less than two years. By commitment, I'm not saying don't live together or be in an exclusive relationship - but marriage, children, buying a house or making any other significant financial commitment should only be considered after you have been together exclusively for two years. You **cannot** be sure that you know the true sense of a person until you have come through the honeymoon period in your relationship (the first 12-18 months) and arrive at the point where the person you see, day in and day out, is the *true self.*

As humans, we do not deliberately set out to 'pretend' to be someone that we are not. However, in the beginning of a relationship our brain is flooded with a variety of hormones that make us behave differently. You need time to allow your brain to settle, for this person to lose their 'novelty' factor in your life and then determine if this is someone that you are happy to be around - for the long term.

If you are with someone who you want to 'change' – get out of the relationship!

I don't mean minor things - like leaving the toilet seat up, or dropping dirty clothes on the floor in front of the laundry basket, but significant behavioural or personality issues. No matter how important you are in a person's life - if they have issues, they are not your issues to fix. Your love will not usually be enough to fix them either; that person has to WANT to fix themself. To knowingly go into a relationship believing that your presence will help fix an issue is just setting yourself up for failure.

You CANNOT change another human being, and you should not WANT to.

If you really want to achieve a loving and nurturing partnership in your life, you first need to examine yourself and understand with great clarity WHO you are and WHAT you want for yourself. When you reach true acceptance of self, then you have space in your life for the other to come in.

This is why I always start with working through your sense of self. You have to know who you truly are and be able to love her before you will find the complement for her. Otherwise, what you take into a relationship is a persona that is looking to the OTHER to make you feel valued and worthwhile. However, what you end up attracting is a partner who believes the same negative things about you that you secretly believe about yourself. The result is that they will perpetuate those negative feelings. This is a sub-conscious process of attraction, in which we are drawn to someone who will manifest more negative beliefs within us.

In this way, human beings are really quite self-destructive.

Oh, I know it doesn't feel that way in the beginning… The honeymoon period is when you are quite literally 'crazy' in love as a result of all of the extra endorphins and neurotransmitters - the brain chemicals that are released when we fall in love. You recall the period in which we can't seem to think about anything else but your new partner. The brain emits extra hormones in response to the novelty of a new partner, and in this way your brain assists you to create a connection - and it feels awesome!

However, you will usually find that the connections that you feel pulling you in the *most strongly* are also the ones that start to twinge your intuitive senses within about three weeks. At this point we usually argue against the intuition because we have no evidence for our feelings, so we justify the connection to ourselves in a multitude of ways.

In contrast, when a potentially good relationship is on the horizon, you may find yourself attracted to this person, but not so strongly connected - at least initially. You may feel like you want to walk away from an opportunity like this - yet in reality, this is probably the right one for you. But something about it doesn't make you FEEL right, because your subconscious is not firing about the potential you have to fix the issues in such a relationship.

Even after you have become clearer about your true sense of self, and a good relationship walks into your life, you will struggle to feel comfortable in it initially. I personally have had classic patterns around this. I am always attracted to partners who need me - they often don't have a good sense of themselves and my love for them initially pumps them up and there is a strong connection. Inevitably though, their own belief in themselves is that they don't deserve me, that I'm too good for them and then they project this onto me, that I make them feel inadequate.

These relationships were doomed from the beginning because I CANNOT fill that void for another human being - they have to want to examine their own life and fill that void for themselves. But I desire to want to fill it for them, because that makes me feel wanted - my ability to give is what makes me feel valuable. In the past my sense of self-worth was always about my ability to GIVE to another human being - but not anymore.

That sounds like I have some sort of ego, but it is quite the opposite. It is just the reflection of me giving too much of myself to another human being when they don't feel deserving of it. In reality, by their own behaviour, they probably don't deserve it, but due to my own need to feel deserving of their love, I do too much for them and don't hold them to account for much in return. This is where I often talk about 1s and 2s in relationship – self nurturers and other nurturers.

I had to understand myself and stop projecting my need to feel worthy by my ability to give to others. Working as a therapist has helped this a lot - I simply cannot give a lot emotionally to a very needy person in my intimate relationship because I am already giving out to many other people through my work. I simply don't have any more to give. A relationship for me now has to give back to me; not totally one way, but it cannot be the kind of relationship I have had in my past.

The statistics around therapists indicates that many of them are single, and I would argue that this is why. However, therapists are people too and they need to be able to be self-aware enough to understand themselves and seek to do things differently. At the end of the day, therapist or not, many people lack the insight or energy to change their situation.

This is why YOU are UNIQUE!

You are taking the time to examine yourself with a view to making change and achieving a different outcome. After all, isn't the definition of insanity performing the same behaviour over and over again and expecting a different outcome? You know you need to do this differently… That's why you are here.

How to Find the Relationship You Desire

Firstly, there are the basics about reviewing your sense of self. Until you can look in the mirror and *truly love* the person you see (and I don't mean physically), you are not ready for a significant other in your life. If you are in a relationship and feel like you want to leave it - I **guarantee** that this is the reason why... You cannot love another human being until you first LOVE yourself. The person you are with will be reflecting back onto you all of the things you don't like about yourself and reinforcing the negative.

This is why I often see clients go through a therapeutic process of their own and subsequently leave their relationship! It is great if a couple can grow together, but often one wants to grow and the other doesn't; a relationship cannot be sustained in this scenario. So if you still can't look at yourself in the mirror and LOVE what you see, or at least acknowledge that you are growing the love you have for yourself - go back to Chapter One and review it.

If you don't like the physical - understand that as a result of the change in how you see yourself, you will stop overeating and using food to manage emotion. We focus on this in Chapter Five, when we look at Health and Wellbeing. If you truly believe you are ready then we are now going to get practical about the steps you need to take to find a truly fulfilling connection and potential relationship.

But please save yourself the angst of **another** failed relationship. You need to do the work on yourself before the universe can bring you what you really need in your life. So please don't move forward until you can honestly say you are happy with WHO you are, when you can say...

"I am deserving"!

Now you are ready to be delectable...

@Daily Reflection

Under the 'Resources' tab on the website, you will find a sheet about 'Daily Reflection'. Please follow the instructions and complete this exercise for yourself and commit yourself to making this part of your daily regime.

Social Interaction

Despite all your wishful thinking - your future partner is NOT going to come knocking on your front door. I have one girlfriend who argues this point with me because she met her partner when he came to her house to buy something she had listed for sale. However, even in that scenario, she had to first take an action to be able to get an interaction.

We often fill our lives with other things to fill the void that not having a partner creates. Sometimes these are good things, but often they are not. Some of us become workaholics - we are so busy with work that we don't have time for anything else. In this way we can delude ourselves into believing that we are too busy for a relationship anyway. In reality, we will always make room in our lives for the things that are important to us. Some of us will fill the void with alternatives, like food or wine. These things often help us to minimise or avoid our emotions.

We need to challenge ourselves to interact in different ways - and I'm not talking about online dating! We need to pursue new interests, connect with social groups, reconnect with friends and actively seek out interaction in DIFFERENT ways to what you are doing now. If you are reading this and saying "I don't have time" - then you are deluding yourself into believing you are ready for a relationship, or even to be happy within yourself.

I'm not saying that you should interact socially in pursuit of a relationship - this is not the purpose of the interaction. In fact, if you are socially interacting solely in pursuit, the interaction will usually be fleeting and often leaves you with a feeling of emptiness. I want you to seek interaction for the sole purpose of connecting with people around the things that you enjoy and are interested in. It is about learning to enjoy life; doing the things that bring you joy.

Hobbies

There are several options, including taking up a class at an adult learning establishment - learn a new language, take a cooking or dance class, or get that camera out of your wardrobe and learn how to use it. Perhaps you have always wanted to learn to paint or draw, learn yoga or meditation or volunteer in a soup kitchen. It doesn't matter what the hobby is - but I want you to find one. Push yourself outside of your comfort zone and do something for the pure joy of doing - get in touch with the creative part of yourself and enjoy the process of creating without judging the outcome.

@MeetUp.com

I recommend that you join MeetUp.com. MeetUp is a worldwide online social network with thousands of different social groups around the world. Where I live, which is a city of 400,000 people, there are more than 200 active social groups on MeetUp.

MeetUp groups range from basic 'social' groups who just get together for drinks or a meal, to movie groups, music groups, walking groups, canine companion groups, photography, dance, meditation and sporting groups… You name it and they appear to have a group for it. There are 'women only' groups and mixed social groups - I want you to join and take yourself along to a MeetUp. Most of the people in MeetUp have come along to an event alone in the past and they are very friendly and engage with new members quite readily.

Yes, there are single people in MeetUp groups - but the purpose is not 'dating' it's 'socialising'. You need to make time in your life for more fun!

To Date or Not to Date… That is the question!

Before you even contemplate dating – we need to undertake an examination of what it is that you actually want for yourself. Don't give me the "I just want someone to love me" bullshit either! You have a LIST - you are just not honest with people about its existence.

@Traits List

In the section on 'Clarifying Our Needs' I asked you to refer to the 'Traits List' (see **Appendix 2**). Now I want you to revisit that list of traits as we are going to determine the traits that you seek in a potential partner. I want you to place a tick next to all of the positive traits that you would like in a future partner. Then I want you to place a tick next to the negative traits that you could tolerate in a potential partner (you must choose at least five). It is a fact that we all have negative things about us

- no partner will be perfect and neither are you. In addition to traits, are there other social requirements – status, finances, children, etc.?

Take time with this exercise as it is very important that you are clear about what you really want in a partner and what you are prepared to compromise on and what you are not. Please complete this now. If you prefer, there is an online assessment that you can do on the website in the 'Resources' area. Complete this and note your Top 10 in your 'Revolutionary Roadmap'.

Only you can honestly answer the question about whether or not you are 'ready' - but if you feel you want to, then go ahead. But remember – just because you connect with someone doesn't mean that you need to date them exclusively. Just try to take it easy and don't play any games. If you like someone, tell them… But try not to put that on them with any pressure. If you can be open and honest about what you would like, you will often find the other person will be open and honest in return.

Be prepared as you WILL fall back into old habits. I guarantee that the first few people you date exclusively will start to ring your old alarm bells within the first two to three weeks. Call it for what it is… Just because you have connected with someone and slept with them, doesn't mean you need to continue in the relationship until it becomes **really** obvious what the problem is.

Be honest with yourself and the person you are dating, they deserve to understand why an interaction may not work for you. Remember, the ownership of that belongs to you - so the rationale for why something isn't working is very much about being clear about what you want and what you don't. You have your list… Don't compromise on it because you will only resent the person for the fact that you made that compromise at some point in your future.

The Pros and Cons of Online Dating

I am not opposed to online dating - in fact, I have done it myself and utilised varying websites to try it out. I have no particular positive or negative perspectives, just some basic rules that I think you need to apply, ensuring that you approach things in full awareness.

Be aware that there are different types of sites. The first category were designed to be 'hook-up' sites, such as Burn or Tinder. You need to be aware that the primary purpose of these sites is to connect you with people looking for sexual interactions; they are not usually the place for people looking for longer-term connections. It's not to say that a sexual interaction may not develop into something else, but it is less likely that the people who have profiles on these sites are looking for more than a physical connection.

Then you have the general dating sites like Match, RSVP, Zoosk, POF, etc. These are often low cost sites where you can connect with people in varying financial ways including by purchasing monthly memberships or tokens for contact. Initially membership is often free, so this can often be an entry point for people into the online dating world, and their desired outcomes can vary from just looking for friendship to desiring a relationship that will result in marriage. They require more active searching of the available profiles and will offer some matching for a fee.Then there are your more expensive online services like eHarmony and Elite Singles. If you are looking for a relationship and seeking to be matched on similar interests or intellect, then these sites allow you to be better matched on personality, values and attributes. However, they usually don't allow you to just look through all of the available people in your area as they filter your matches based on the defined parameters of your profile, which are determined by the assessment process that you undertake when you become a member of their site. So it is important to be aware that unless you live in quite a large city with a population of a few million, there are often not many people who are members of the site that you are able to be matched with, who also live close by.

The main thing to remember is that online dating can be helpful because you know that the people on the site are usually looking for a connection. However, different people are looking for differing types of connection, so be aware that you may find that some sites are a bit of a 'meat market' and that can make you feel devalued if you are searching for the love of your life. Finding the most appropriate dating site for your needs is important. You have to match your desired outcome with the right site.

@Why Men Are Like Shoes

Under the 'Resources' tab on the website you will find a link to a reading of my book "Why Men Are Like Shoes". In this book I take a very cheeky look at the world of dating and why you need to be clear about what you are looking for if you want to ensure that your wardrobe contains your perfect pair of shoes!

You can't shop for a pair of Jimmy Choo shoes in Target, nor can you find a great pair of running shoes in Saks 5th Ave. You need to know what type of shoes you are looking for and make sure you have gone to the right type of store to buy them, so your choice of which online dating site to sign up to requires some thought and research.

Look out for your copy of 'Why Men Are Like Shoes' in mid-2017.

@How I Hacked Online Dating by Amy Webb

I encourage you to look at the Ted Talk by Amy Webb:

http://www.ted.com/talks/amy_webb_how_i_hacked_online_dating

Not that I am anticipating that you will need to go to the extreme lengths that Amy did, and in all likelihood you don't have the skills or resources to do it, but it is a great laugh in any case… It highlights the challenges of online dating and the things you need to consider. However, like most things, I think you need to approach the whole process with an open mind. Just anticipate that you will need to kiss many frogs before you find your Prince, so be prepared for it to take time and don't rush…

Children

Children are an important consideration in any relationship. Whether you have children or not, consideration needs to be given to what you want in your future life regarding children. When I first started dating again, I was newly divorced with young children; they were six and eight. I always sought to date someone who had children around a similar age, as it made it easier to navigate life and you had similar responsibilities and freedoms.

I have walked away from good relationships because of the differing responsibilities around children, and I have walked away from bad relationships because of the impact on my children. I have compromised on this in the past, for really rational reasons, and I found out the hard way that this adds extra pain on both sides. Now that my children are grown up I will not date someone with young children.

My Thoughts

Yes, I feel selfish in even saying it to myself, let alone admitting it here in black and white. In some ways, my decision could be viewed as selfish. However, I feel like I have done my job, raised my children and, now that they have left home, I am enjoying my freedom. I travel and I socialise and if I feel like eggs on toast for dinner, I can eat it without guilt. I eat out more because I can afford to and I like it. These things are more important to me than a relationship.

Perhaps it is because I know that there are many good people out there in differing life stages, not all of their life circumstances are going to suit me, nor mine them. Because I am secure in myself, I can walk away from a connection; as I know that I don't need a relationship so badly that I will compromise my own personal desires to achieve it. I have learned that to do so will only backfire in the end, as you come to resent the compromise you had to make… Especially if you don't feel that you are given anything in return. It tips the scales out of balance.

Financial Agreements

This is one of the other areas where I no longer compromise. I honestly don't care what another person has in terms of assets, or what they do in terms of their level of income, but I am not prepared to expose my own financial security for the connection.

I am very open with any prospective partner about the need for a financial agreement to be set-up within the first six months of a relationship. It doesn't matter whether you live together or not. In Australia, you can claim an emotional dependence even when you do not live under the same roof. For this reason, I say you need to provide yourself with some basic protection, and you need to organise this without emotional involvement. I have seen many people who are SO afraid of losing their assets that they cut themselves off to the possibility of love… It is not necessary.

You just need to complete a basic agreement and get independent legal advice before signing it. If your partner refuses because "If you love someone you should trust them" - run! If they truly loved you they would seek to protect you from harm, even if that harm came from them at a future point in time. It's not personal - it's practical and it can avoid a whole lot of emotional torture and financial costs down the track.

@Financial Agreement – Basic

I want you to go to the 'Resources' area on the website and you will find a basic checklist for what a financial agreement should contain. This type of agreement is very simple and doesn't consider children or other complexities, but I want you to try and understand the basic premise. If you end up in a relationship with someone who has good financial security, you can't expect to walk away from that relationship with any of their good fortune - even if they behaved badly. In return, they cannot have any such expectations of you. If you both make this clear from the outset and confirm it in writing, then nothing should go wrong… If it does, then at least the financial outcome is clear.

Regardless, most financial arguments post-separation are about trying to punish the other and they are driven by emotional pain. If we can remove the potential for this as an option, any separation will be more readily worked through.

Are You Ready?

So, I have outlined a number of considerations that need to be made in contemplation of whether or not you are ready to seek a new relationship. Moving forward, only you can decide if you're ready. When we are fully accepting of ourselves, we can remove the barriers inside us that hold us back from love…

Then we will no longer need to seek love outside of ourselves… It will come to us, and flow through us, because we have cleared the path for it to flood our lives.

You will be Delectable…

Decisive Diva

Let's look at your future...

I believe that we can be honest, true to our own quirky nature and be fully and openly accepted anyway...

Chapter Three

How is your career tracking for you? Are you at a place in your working life where you are doing something that you absolutely love? Or have you reached a place in your career where you feel stuck? There are multiple scenarios that can impact how we feel about our working life, so I'm going to try to do my best to cover them, noting that it is rather challenging to be all things to all people when trying to understand the multiple working environments and factors that impact our perception of work.

But let me ask you a few things...

Do you feel satisfied that your career is at a place where you are on the right path for yourself?

Are you satisfied with the working hours that you are doing? Do you have enough time for family, friends and leisure activities?

Do you feel that you missed your opportunity to do what you are REALLY passionate about?

If you answered yes to any of these, then keep reading as we are going to work out how to make your working life more rewarding. Firstly, the main issue to understand is whether or not your career path chose you, or you chose it. I have worked with many executive clients over the years. They all find that in the middle of their life they feel that they have reached a pinnacle in their careers but they feel very unhappy and dissatisfied.

Consideration needs to be given to what you truly want from life. We often believe that career success will result in life satisfaction, and yet they are two very different constructs. Have you achieved career success? If so, are you happy and satisfied with your life? If these questions just raise more questions, we need to examine what to do about the issues.

Passion

Are you passionate about your work? Most of us work in our role for seven to eight hours per day for at least five days per week - that's most of your waking life. Do you enjoy work - or do you endure it?

For ease of understanding, I will give you the age range for generational cohorts as I interpret them – there is much debate about referencing generations, I relay my personal perspective here that follows an approximate 15-year timeframe for each generation.

Baby boomers (post WWII to mid 1960's) as a generation have what is commonly called a Protestant work ethic. They trained for a role and then worked in that role for most of their lives, often with the same company. Gen Xers (mid 1960's to early 80's) change careers about every 10 years on average. There are some exceptions to this based on occupation - doctors are a classic example of this, where the main reason why they don't change roles has to do with the length of time it takes to train to become a doctor. Many health based occupations are the same.

Gen Ys (early 80's to mid 90's) are more likely to change career every three to five years. If not their career, then certainly their employer. They seek to travel much more than earlier generations, they seek to move up the ranks in their career quickly and if they don't get what they want, they move on. This is quite challenging for both the employee and the employer. Millennials (mid 90's to 2010) are now moving into the full-time workforce and they appear to be even less stable than Gen Y.

As our society has become more educated and aware due to the information overload that we are now experiencing, many opportunities abound. Young people are more prepared to take risks - part of that is also because they have less to lose and less responsibility. My research has shown that most of my readers will be in the Baby boomer or Gen X group. However, there are always exceptions.

We often believe that career success will result in life satisfaction...

It doesn't!

They are two completely separate constructs

Due to a number of factors, this makes you less inclined to take risks in your career… We approach life with a 'Better the Devil You Know' attitude. However, this often is our biggest stumbling block when we are unhappy in our work - as we are too scared to take risks.

Let's go through a number of exercises designed to look at your current situation, your natural personality traits and how they impact the things that you are good at. We will look at what your real passions are and how you may be able to factor these into your working life so that you may feel more overall satisfaction with life.

Current Work Review

- Do you currently work for someone else?
- Are you full-time or part-time?
- Do your hours suit you and your lifestyle?
- If not, how much money do you need to be able to manage your commitments?
- How many hours per week would you need to work to meet these commitments?
- What are you prepared to give up in order to make a change in your life?

@Personality Profile Assessment

I would like you to complete a 'Personality Profile Assessment'. You will need to log in to the 'Membership' area on the website, click on the link and complete the online assessment. Be sure to note your result in your 'Revolutionary Roadmap'.

Role

What does the result of your personality profile say about the type of role you should be filling in your life? Are you working to your strengths? Often people who are very unhappy in their working life are working in areas or on tasks that are quite opposite to their natural strengths - this is why they are SO unhappy.

Do you need to make a change? If so, what sort of change should it be? Does a change require further education? If so, how would you go about achieving this? Are you prepared to make the commitment to the process of change? Because if you are not ready, you will just be setting yourself up to fail - and no one wants that.

If money was not a consideration, what would you most like to be doing with your waking hours?

My Career Just Needs a Tweak

If you are happy in your career generally but you would like to make some minor changes to your current situation - perhaps in hours, location, employer, upper management, etc., then perhaps your career just needs a tweak.

My Career Needs a Complete Overhaul

One of the most challenging issues when you are really unhappy in your job is to understand how you are going to make the change you need. The first question to ask yourself is 'What do I want to do?'

For many of us, even if we know what we would prefer to be doing, we don't have a clear idea about how to make a significant change, or it feels like you left it too late to make a big change, but I would encourage you to reconsider your perspective. Do you have a particular passion?

The Value of Education

When I was considering options for a career change, I knew that education was going to have to be at the base of my decision. As a young woman, I was working in the finance sector and I had been recognised within that as a potential high flyer. At 19 years of age, the bank I worked for sent me off on a special weekend for people they had identified with talent. I was the youngest person in the group and the only one who had not finished high school.

The bank's head economist gave us a talk and, being the naturally curious human being that I am, I asked questions and engaged him in discussion. At the end of his session he approached me and asked if I had done economics in my senior school studies - I explained that I had never studied economics and I had actually never finished high school. He was surprised, but told me that I had a natural head for economics and that if I would go to university to study economics, the bank would pay for everything and he would personally sign off on my study application.

I was amazed! This was not the first time that someone had appreciated my work or my willingness to be open and engage with a topic of learning, but it was the first time anyone of power and influence had truly recognised that talent and put their money where their mouth was.

This was the first true recognition of me as an individual, and I really took it to heart.

So, I found myself actively researching how I could get into university, which school was the best for studying economics, and trying to work out how I was going to do that without completing my senior studies. I was 20 years old. I spoke with the student advisor at a university who told me that I could apply to university as a mature student at 21. She also advised that if I wanted to demonstrate my aptitude for the subject matter, it may help if I undertook some study during that year whilst I was waiting out my time. So, I enrolled to study senior economics at night school.

For a year, I took myself off to my local adult education centre and studied economics. I found the subject matter engaging and I rather enjoyed the challenge of learning something that had some applicability to my working life, albeit at some point in my future. I scored 95% in my final mark for that unit! I thought I had found my calling - something I was really good at and could excel in.

So, then I applied to university and was accepted. In the meantime, I had become a little disillusioned with my working life. See, the bank really thought I had talent and they wanted to nurture it. However, this was still the days of the Protestant work ethic, where you were expected to stay working for the same organisation, or at least in the same sector, for your whole career.

I am a Generation-X member. We were the first to decide that when life got boring you could move on. We were raised by mothers who came through the sexual revolution of the 60s. They told us that we didn't have to be like them - we could do and be anything we wanted to be. Also, when we chose to become mothers, we would still be able to have our careers. We were the generation raised to believe that we really could 'have our cake and eat it too'!

So… I was bored at the bank. I had talent, they told me, I was going to go places. I had been earmarked for a great career in the bank. However, I would have to wait four to five years working in my front line customer service role before any of these opportunities would really start to come my way… I had to earn my stripes, do my time and work my way up the food chain utilising the old 'time = seniority' rule.

Well, this approach just didn't suit me. I'm a little impatient at the best of times and I'm a big believer in being directly rewarded for effort. Around this time, I came across my first entrepreneurial opportunity, so I did what most young people without fear do - I worked hard to save money to train in a new skill and then I left my stable and secure job in the finance sector and embarked on my first business venture. It was 1991.

If you are Australian, some of you who are reading this will recall that this was the beginning of the *'recession we had to have'*. When I put in my notice at the bank, I was summoned to see the head of HR in head office and she tried to talk me out of my decision. She told me that Australia was going to be experiencing some difficult times in the very near future and that I really should stay in my secure 9-5 job and not take a big risk at that time.

But I was young, I had the world at my feet and I was not naturally inclined to be 'risk averse'. So… I thanked her very much for her concern and resigned anyway. Like most new businesses and first time business owners, my business failed in the first 12 months. However, as any great entrepreneur will tell you, it is in failing that you learn the most.

When I left the bank they had told me that they would always keep a door open for me. Unfortunately, when I went back to them and asked for another opportunity 12 months later, their hands were tied, due to a recruitment freeze that lasted a couple of years. The only work I could get at this time was a part-time role, job-sharing in a different bank for two days per week. I took it because I needed the money. I was able to increase my hours from there, but I was unable to work more than 25 hours per week for almost three years.

Strangely enough, I had still gone through with my application to university and been offered a place studying a Bachelor of Economics. For a number of reasons, I found that university level economics was different - I really enjoyed and excelled in one area, but got frustrated and confused with the other. After six months I ended up deferring because I was pregnant with my first child. By the time I was due to go back, I didn't feel that economics was right for me. I knew I wanted to study, but I needed to spend some time working out 'what'.

I had gone to university because someone else had believed in me and thought that I would be really good at economics. However, this was a classic example of how sometimes we 'fall' into a career - not by choice or a clarity of our own passion or sense of purpose, but because someone else put an opportunity in front of us and we didn't have any other ideas.

But it wasn't really ME…

Whilst home with my baby I started to do some work with a community consultant and really started to think about what interested me. It was during this time (my second pregnancy) that I decided that what I was really passionate about was people, in particular young people. I still remembered what it was like to be a teenager and I was interested in working with young people. I also recalled that I had really enjoyed working with my school counsellor at high school, so I decided I wanted to become a school counsellor.

In order to be a school counsellor I had to study psychology. This is how I came to return to study when my youngest daughter was 12 months old; this time undertaking a Bachelor of Science (Psychology). It took me 11 years to complete my undergraduate degree. I studied part-time and worked full-time for most of those years and I was also a sole parent for the majority of it. I commenced my studies as an off-campus student, but after eight years I transferred to be an on-campus student. This was a critical shift in my education as I had hit third year and I was struggling with motivation and understanding the new material. I really needed to be able to interact with lecturers and other students to assist me to learn new concepts.

In order to even be considered to work as a psychologist, I needed to complete Honours - another two years part-time. Then I had to work as an intern for two years - this was working for an organisation with no financial remuneration. So, I cut back my full-time paid work hours and worked full-time for free and another 25 hours a week in my government job to feed and clothe us.

Finally, 15 years after I first embarked on my studies in Psychology, I became a Registered Psychologist. This is now the field in which I work full-time; I have my own psychology practice and I am able to make a difference every day. I followed my passion and this allows me to live a fulfilled life in terms of my work. Although I am constantly looking for new things to do and ways to improve my working life, I firmly believe that this is the outpouring of the entrepreneurial spirit within me.

So, why did I share my life story with you? I want you to understand that sometimes the path to career satisfaction is not necessarily straightforward. You need to have a passion to commit yourself to the process, because life is going to do its best to get in the way. If you don't have clarity of purpose and a strong desire to do something different, you will not have the dedication to see it through.

What was really interesting was that during all of the years I was studying, my career path also improved. My decision to continue my studies and see through my ultimate goal was not about money. I was earning extremely good money when I left my job to go out on my own as a full-time psychologist. But I had a dedication to see my dream fulfilled and I had worked so hard to get there, I had to take the risk and see it through.

Tenacity

I will admit, there were many times I thought about giving up, especially around the eight-year mark, which was when I moved to being an on-campus student. I was just finding it too difficult to motivate myself on my own, and it was especially difficult to try to explore concepts when I was not attending a class. I am an auditory learner - understanding how you learn is an extremely important piece of information to know about yourself. Walter Burke Barbe and his colleagues[5] proposed three learning modalities - visual, auditory and kinesthetic (often identified by the acronym VAK).

Then, Neil Fleming[6] expanded on their work and outlined that visual learners have a preference for seeing (visual aids that represent ideas using methods other than words, such as graphs, charts, diagrams, symbols, etc). Auditory learners best absorb information through listening (lectures, discussions, tapes, etc). Tactile/kinesthetic learners prefer to learn via experience - moving, touching, and doing (active exploration of the world, science projects, experiments, etc). You can use this model to identify your preferred learning style and maximise your learning by focusing on the mode that seems to benefit you the most.

5 Barbe, W B; Swassing, R H; Milone, M N (1979) *Teaching through modality strengths: concepts and practices*. Zaner-Bloser, Columbus, Ohio.

6 Fleming, Neil D (2014) *The VARK modalities*. vark-learn.com

As an auditory learner I needed to interact with others, hear the discussion and be able to ask questions in order to absorb information. If I had not been able to transfer to an on-campus study option, I believe I may have given up. There were also other things that life threw at me during those 15 years that made me question myself and whether or not it was all worth it. There were times I doubted myself, when I felt like a bad mother because I had competing priorities around my children. It was especially difficult without a partner to support me in time and resources - the sacrifices I made around my personal life were significant.

I had the strongest desire to improve myself - both for myself and for my children. I firmly believed that I needed to do this to improve our lives and I did. I'm not sure my children really understood this when they were growing up. I know, for a fact, that my youngest resented being dragged into my lectures when she was sick because I couldn't afford to miss a lecture. However, I'm sure she now understands why I did it, even if she doesn't agree with the impact it had on her life, in terms of her perceived lack of attention from me because I was always busy - and I still am.

I really hope that my adult children now understand that my dedication to my own self-improvement was for my own benefit, but also to improve their lives as well. I hope that my tenacity in persevering through all of the things that life threw at me during those years really taught them to have purpose, passion and drive. If I have allowed my children to 'learn what they live' - then I believe I have been the best mother that I could be.

Commit to DO Something

It is a well-known phenomenon that when we set goals and review them regularly, we are much more likely to achieve them.

@Future Template

In the 'Resources' area on the website, locate the 'Future Template'. Complete this and note your result in your 'Revolution Roadmap'. Please remember to continue to complete the 'Daily Reflection' to support your vision.

May I also encourage you to create a visual representation of your 'Future Template' (create a vision board using a range of images and put it up somewhere prominent) and share your future plans with the significant people in your life - your mentor, partner, close family and friends and also with your fellow Divas in our Private Facebook Group.

@Accountability Muse

Your next step is to go into our Private Facebook Group, this is only for women like yourself who buy my book, or engage with my programs. I would like you to introduce yourself to the group and then ask if one of the other group members would like to be your 'Accountability Muse'.

This will be one of the other 'Gorgeous Girls' in our clan, who will also need an 'Accountability Muse' - you will support each other. You need to commit to the regular review and reflection of your 'Future Template' - diarise a time at the beginning of each month to have a quick online or phone chat to check your progress.

You have clarity...

You have purpose...

You have dedication...

You are Decisive!
Let's get on with it Gorgeous

Discerning Diva

Let's talk about money...

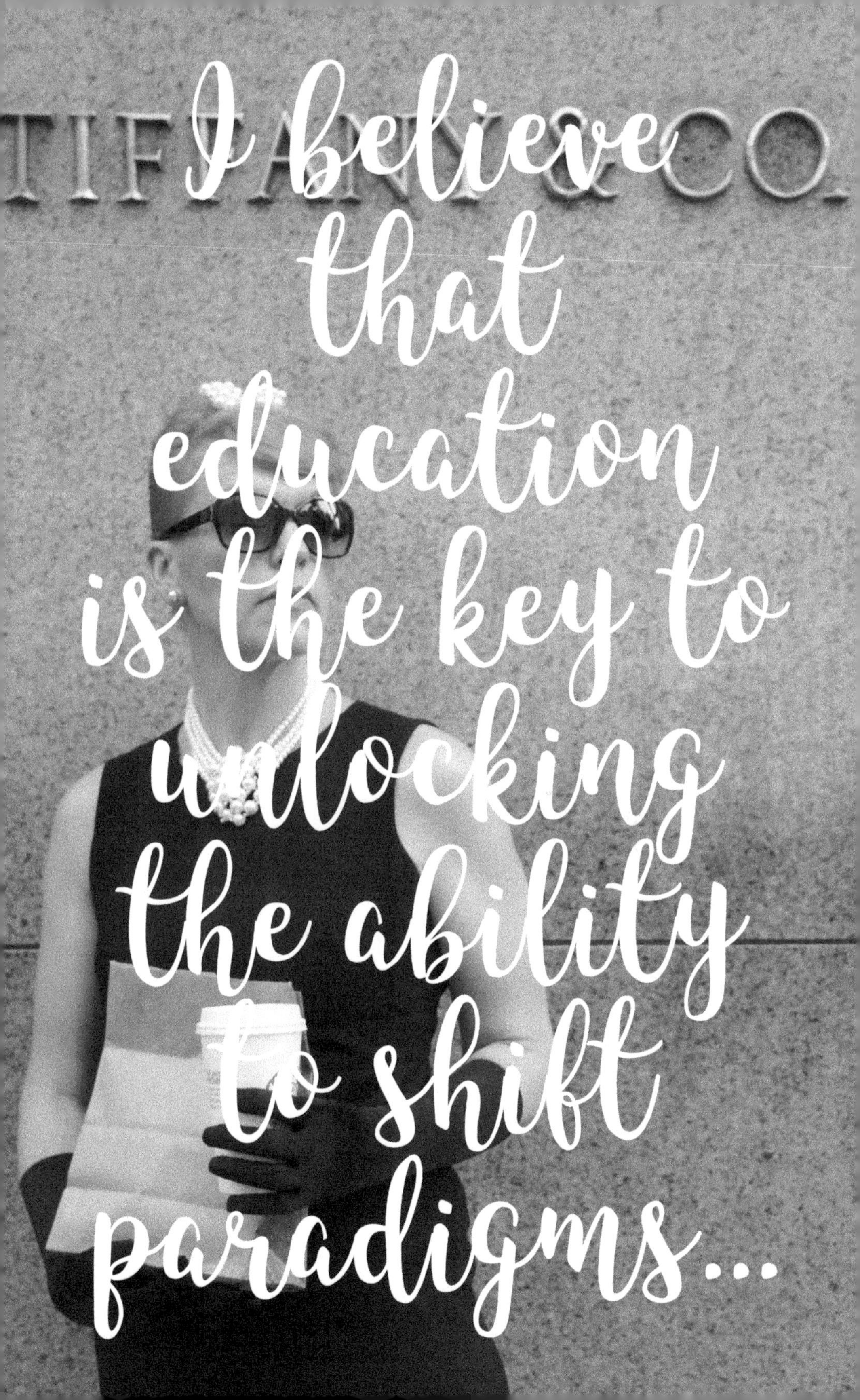

I believe that education is the key to unlocking the ability to shift paradigms...

Chapter Four

Most of us completely underestimate the impact of money on our lives. As women, we often sacrifice our own financial needs and desires for our loved ones, including partners, children and extended family. We don't seek to gather wealth like men do - perhaps this is because of our natural tendency to nurture and care for others, our general tendency for self-sacrifice. Or perhaps it is about our feelings of 'deservedness'.

All too-often we end up in our mid-life not as financially secure as we would like. If you have been through a divorce, this could be an even bigger issue. As women who come through divorce, we can often develop a willingness to work ourselves to the bone to maintain the security of a roof over our heads, especially if we have care of our children.

So why do we tend to put our own financial needs last? Why is it that even when we are on good incomes, we find that it never seems to go far enough and we are always trying to make ends meet. The more you have, the more you spend, and yet life still seems to be a little 'empty'.

Let's look at what happens to our mindset when we don't think very highly of ourselves… Remember back in Chapter One where we looked at the belief systems we held about ourselves? You will recall that a lot of the negative beliefs stem from a feeling that we 'don't deserve…' - insert 'blank' here!

How can we create **abundance** in our lives when we approach it with a scarcity mindset?

Singledom

Many modern women in western societies who have divorced find themselves in a place where they have total financial freedom but maybe not a significant asset base. Alternatively, perhaps you have dedicated yourself to your career and done well for yourself in building an asset base, but potentially sacrificed other things in the process.

It is always easier, from a financial perspective, to live in 'shared' space than to live alone - it's simple mathematics because shared resources reduce the costs on both parties. So if you have spent a lot of time as a single woman, particularly living alone or with your children, then your ability to accumulate wealth will have been significantly affected.

Shared Assets? Partnerships...

What if you are in a relationship and you have shared assets? Or you may be single and have some shared assets with family members or other friends. In any case, you need to understand your own asset pool, your liabilities and what your financial goals are in order to implement a plan to change and improve them.

The challenge in any form of partnership is: "What happens if you want different financial outcomes to the person that you're partnered with and you need to leverage your assets to improve your position?" This is a challenge, and one that is not easily addressed, as you need to be really clear on the nature of the relationship between the parties, the separation of finances, the separation of labour in the partnership and a range of other things before this can be clarified.

I can't answer all of those issues for you here, but suffice to say that if you are 'tied' to a financial partner who does not share your financial goals, at some point in your future you are going to need to sever that financial partnership.

Financial Agreements – The Basics

There is a reason that I highlight the need for financial agreements - mostly this is about protecting your assets from lawyers, but it is also about minimising any emotional difficulties that can be exacerbated by financial differences.

When we fall in love, we don't usually ask people about their financial position - it's considered to be rude. However, if you are even contemplating a long-term relationship with someone, you need to understand their financial position and their approach. This is even more critical if the relationship is early on in your life, as there are a number of issues around children, primary care for children, home ownership and income-splitting that are going to be critical to the long-term effectiveness of the relationship.

As much as we don't like to admit it, marriage and other long-term intimate relationships are really business partnerships with sex thrown in. If you do not have shared goals and values around money, children, the accumulation of wealth and working roles, you are really just setting yourself up for failure.

When you are older and contemplating future relationships (possibly post- divorce), these issues are even more critical. The last thing you need is to feel that your assets or financial stability are at risk - especially if you have children. I don't want to labour this point too much here - I have already outlined it in Chapter Two - but suffice to say, you need to deal with this issue to minimise the impact on your future happiness.

Are you Happy?

It's a funny question to ask around money - are you happy with your current financial position? Most people will say 'No' - but they have no plan in place to change their situation, they merely continue their daily slog and complain about it. I would encourage you to think carefully about your 'real' answer to this question, because money represents different things to different people.

There are many amongst us who seek merely to have the stability of a secure roof over our heads, this is quite an important financial goal for many. However, others would prefer to be able to have a lot of disposable income for travel and don't want to be tied down to the demands of bricks and mortar and the responsibilities that brings.

There is no 'right or wrong' - it is such a personal and individual decision that no one could be expected to answer it definitively. Over the course of your life, your financial goals will also change. So, much like the other areas of your life, you will need to regularly review your position and your goals. This is especially true if you are quite unhappy with your financial position.

Let me give you some insight…

I grew up in a household where we didn't have a lot of money. I remember in my late primary school years that things started to improve around our family finances. Mum had re-educated herself and was now working full-time. There were a couple of my siblings who were now working and contributing, or living out of home, so Mum had fewer costs.

In my early-teens, we moved interstate and it took Mum a while to find work. There was only really one job in town that she was qualified to do and she managed to secure that job for a few years. However, things changed and it got quite difficult for a while when Mum found herself out of work and we moved back into poverty for a few years. I did not move out of poverty until I started working myself… Even then, it took a while for me to adjust my thinking.

I still remember as a teenager begging my mother to pay an extra $8 to allow me to have a pair of $20 running shoes instead of the $12 ones she was going to buy me - just so I didn't get teased at school for being SO poor that I had to wear supermarket running shoes! I wore my Dunlop Volleys with pride until they were completely worn out. As an adolescent, I was affected by a sense of judgement and stigma and my need to 'belong', as most adolescents are. I did my best to live with my situation, but with some minor compromises to facilitate my existence without TOO much shame. But I knew I was poor… And I knew I wanted to improve my situation to ensure that I didn't have to remain that way.

When I was almost 16 we moved again, to be closer to my sister who had a son with cerebral palsy. This was to another country area that still didn't allow Mum the opportunity to fully utilise her skills and education, but she sacrificed her financial stability to support her family - so typical of many mothers. It was not until we had all left home that my mother made another interstate move, again for family reasons - but this time was out of care and concern for her own mother. This is also indicative of the 'Circle of Life' for us as women - we sacrifice our own needs and desires for our children, and then in our later life we switch caring for children to caring for our parents… But STILL caring!

This move also had an impact on my mother's ability to put her intellect, skills and education to good use - but this time for the better. She was now in a place where she could amalgamate some of her skill sets and commit herself to a more intense position in terms of her time. As a result, she secured a good position, worked hard and was recognised and promoted quickly, thus heralding another 'new phase' in her financial life. However, once again, there were things that she could have done to improve her own financial position, but in the end she accumulated assets for herself and then ended up giving them away.

As a result of my upbringing, my approach to money was a little confused. I didn't know how to save and I didn't know what it was like to own many things. As a child, every time we moved house my mother threw things away, after all 'stuff' is expensive to move. As a result, as an adult I sought to buy many things and I accumulated them. Some people call it hoarding, but for me it was about being able to live in my history. As an adult, I used to lament the loss of my history that I experienced from regularly moving.

I had also grown up in an unstable environment - moving houses and schools a lot. I had a very strong desire to ensure that I never moved my children, as I believed that many of the issues I experienced growing up were as a direct result of moving all the time and the lack of 'connection' to anything tangible.

The effect on my finances as an adult was really interesting.

One of the things that I learned very early on was that if I didn't educate myself then I was never going to be able to change my status in life. It is one of the true blessings in my life that I grew up in a country that allowed me unfettered access to education; in a society that did not judge me based on my family circumstances, but rather on my achievements.

So - I was free to enhance, improve and change. Almost from the moment I left school to start working, I recognised that I needed to keep learning if I wanted to improve. I worked and studied from the time I left school at age 16, almost continuously until I turned 40! There were a few short breaks in there, around children and a few other life events, but on the whole I studied a whole range of things part-time whilst working, always seeking to improve my situation but also with a view to finding some happiness in my working life by training myself in areas that I was interested in.

Through education I was able to alter my financial position. I was able to secure higher paying positions and this provided me greater ability to borrow funds to improve my overall position. However, it seemed that as much as I continued to increase my income - like my mother before me - the increased income always didn't translate into an improved financial position. The more I earned, the more I spent and the more I 'gave away'.

Now don't misunderstand me, I am happy to share my resources with family and friends. However, I was also still trying to fill a void within myself that I thought could be filled with 'stuff'. I had managed to ensure that I maintained the roof over my head when I divorced; it was essential to me that I did so for the security of my children. I then set about trying to fill this space with 'stuff' - the stuff that would ground me, make me feel stable and secure.

But it was just 'stuff' - and in the end it becomes a noose around your neck. I was seeking to use my finances to buy more 'stuff' to make me feel secure, but it also made me feel weighed down. When I reached the point where I was able to gain a full acceptance of myself, and delight in myself as a human being, I no longer needed to accumulate 'stuff'.

I could let it go… Because it no longer 'defined' my worth in this world.

Now I don't want to sound like I'm a monk (letting go of all the ties to material possessions), because that's just not where I am at. I enjoy life's luxuries and I indulge in them, but I now tend to purchase only that which I first **need** and then make a choice based on the 'desire' within that need.

These days, I tend to make the act of purchasing much slower. I used to be impulsive and shop for entertainment. These days, I only shop out of necessity and I take time to research the available things to fill the need and work out what I desire within that.

As a result, I have more money.

Feeling Secure

It is important to understand the security that is provided by finances. If you have ever been out of work, or found that you had to leave your home situation, then you have tasted the bitterness of financial insecurity. As a result, many of us will not take a risk and will often stay in a situation that is making us very unhappy due to the fear of not being financially secure.

When we reach
the point where
we have full
acceptance of
self...
When we can
delight in self as
a human being...
We no longer need
to accumulate
'stuff'

So how do we overcome our need for financial security? Do we really need to overcome it? If it is fuelling your negative feelings about yourself - then yes, it has to change.

There are a number of factors that need to be considered to adjust our approach to finances. We need to understand our financial background, how we grew up and how it impacts our decision making today. We need to look at whether we have supportive financial partners - not just intimate partners, but family, friends and our bankers. However, if the fear of losing an asset is what keeps you in an intimate relationship (even if you are very unhappy), then is there an alternative to be considered - such as a 'non-intimate' partnership?

Many of us get so caught up in the road blocks in our financial position that we miss the opportunity to 'go off-road'. We often think that the only solution is another intimate relationship, and yet it would be better if we kept the intimacy out of our finances. We need to stop using our heart to guide financial issues - money is not the space of mystics; it is the space of scholars. We need to prevent our heart from negotiating any financial decisions.

When I was young I was a terrible impulse buyer; I would often make a purchasing decision on the *spur of the moment* - I would go with my gut. This was as true for small purchases as it was for large ones, but it burned me several times! After a while I realised that I made purchases with my heart and our finances should not be managed by anything other than our head.

That is not to say that I don't purchase the things that I want or desire - I do… But I no longer do it impulsively. If I decide that I **really** want a new dress, pair of shoes, handbag, mobile phone, new computer, furniture or car, or anything in which my decision will be based on looks or design, rather than functionality, I now do my research and I ALWAYS walk away.

Why you should always walk away

I learned the hard way about walking away from a particular vehicle purchase that I made with my fiancé when I was 21 years old. I just went to **look** at bigger cars - my fiancé wanted a larger car, but the car that we were driving around in was mine and it was good enough for a couple and I owned it outright. Our other vehicle was a motorbike.

We were young and naive. I got caught in the old trick of not being able to leave the salesman's office until we signed on the dotted line. A bad move, a bad financial decision and one that would leave me resentful for quite some time. In the end though, I had to **own** the decision. I signed the documents and allowed my heart to be coerced into giving my partner what he desired, even though it didn't fit with my own needs or values.

That was the first time that I realised that I allowed my *heart* into my financial space. I made the same mistake on multiple occasions over many years. In other relationships and different purchases, I have berated myself for the stupidity of allowing myself to be **led** into these decisions. But ultimately, they were my decisions and I had to own them.

When I got very clear that I would no longer allow my heart to lead my financial decisions, I found that my partners were unhappy about this. You see, they were still living in the finances and heart space, and I wasn't. However, they also perceived that my unwillingness to just let my heart take control was perceived as a lack of love for them, as I was not supportive of their desires. They judged me for not being in the same level of financial consciousness that they were in.

But I can no longer be involved with a partner who is on a different level of consciousness around financial issues - the impact is too negative on my heart. So, I choose to be very open with potential partners and up front about my approach to money. If they have a different perspective, I can respect that, but I don't compromise on this issue anymore. I can't - it creates too many opportunities for dissension.

Money Attitude

There are a number of other strategies that I have adopted around money as well. When I was still a young Mum at home with young children, I saw Suzi Ormond on Oprah one day and she was talking about having **respect** for your money, regardless of the amount that you have. She talked about the simplicity of lining up all of the money in your wallet in its 'right' place - denomination order and with a level of respect shown to it. In her mind, if you didn't respect the money that you had, why would the universe seek to give you more? The idea appealed to the former banker in me and I started making sure I did this, and I continue to do it to this day. My financial position has continued to improve ever since.

Now some people may just see that as coincidence or luck. However, I choose to believe that rather than it being down to luck, I respected my money and I had prepared myself for a number of different opportunities through education and taking action. The overall improvement in finances will not happen as a result of only one action; it will be a continued improvement that results from the synergy of a number of actions on your part.

We also need to know how to roll with change.

Self-Employment

I recently had some challenges in borrowing money due to the change in my situation when I chose to give up my well-paying 'secure' job and strike out on my own. For some reason, banks seem to think that as I am now 'self-employed' I am a big risk for lending purposes. This is despite the fact that I have a reasonably large asset pool and I am a professional with a good client base. I find this very frustrating as I am able to furnish my staff with evidence of their earnings and this satisfies their risk, but me managing my own finances appears to be riskier. Surely I'm the one who is going to work the hardest in my business and that would make me the best 'risk' to support… But apparently not.

Again, this is about rules and risk management that have been established in a patriarchal society. Traditionally women in business aren't supported in the same way that men are. In my experience, men and women do not have to adhere to the same set of rules. Those who assess criteria for lending appear to be more flexible with men in business, or with women in business who are supported by husbands with 'real' jobs, rather than independent, intelligent, single women.

Having said that, after several difficult interactions with a number of large financial institutions, I did approach the Commonwealth Bank and challenged them to put their 'money where their mouth is'. They have a support network called *'Women In Focus'* and they regularly run events in the major capital cities and support groups like Business Chicks. So, I was connected to a Senior Business Home Lending Specialist (even the fact that they have such a position was impressive) and she worked closely with me to sort out all of my business and personal banking needs. She

My Thoughts

personally facilitated introductions to other specialists within the bank to address all of my requirements, and they came out to my office to discuss my needs. As a result of this exceptionally personalised service - I have moved from five banks to one! All my business and personal banking needs met and streamlined, and she assisted me to free up my cash flow - which in business is crucial. Overall, this was the most positive experience I have ever had with a financial institution.

So - there are a few issues we need to consider in managing our finances.

Firstly, there is planning for your future. It is important that we seek the services of a good financial advisor at least once every two years. We need to plan for our future and the future of our children. We need to consider life insurance, wills, superannuation, investment strategies and long term goals. Most of us seek security in the property in which we reside, but next to that we often do very little in terms of taking care of ourselves through financial planning in the long term.

In Australia, we have compulsory superannuation. However, many of us only ever contribute the minimum amount. Especially if you are partnered and take time out to raise children, the focus on superannuation for women is really not there. In divorce, many women seek to gain the best settlement and often engage lawyers in the hope of getting a better outcome, including some level of superannuation split. However, they often lose any potential financial gain by paying it out in legal fees.

Many law firms exist by promoting a collaboration model, seemingly to save you money by negotiating outside of court. What this usually means is that they send each other many letters to keep you out of court - which often utilises more of their time and resources, thereby costing more money than if you just filed in court in the first place. I recognise that sometimes legal processes can not be avoided, I have been involved with a couple myself, but often they are emotionally driven and that ends up costing everyone involved.

@Basic Financial Review

On the website in the 'Membership' area there is a document called 'Financial Review'. Please complete this now. When you have done this, please note your results in your 'Revolution Roadmap'.

This document will help provide you with the snapshot that you need to assess your current financial position and provide some insight into what you should do next to grow your assets, reduce your liabilities and improve your overall wealth position in the future. I'm not a financial planner, so I don't profess this process is financial advice - it is a review process of your 'Life' and that includes your financial position.

You are Discerning...
You are Deserving!

Divine Diva

Let's talk about health and wellbeing... From a psychological perspective

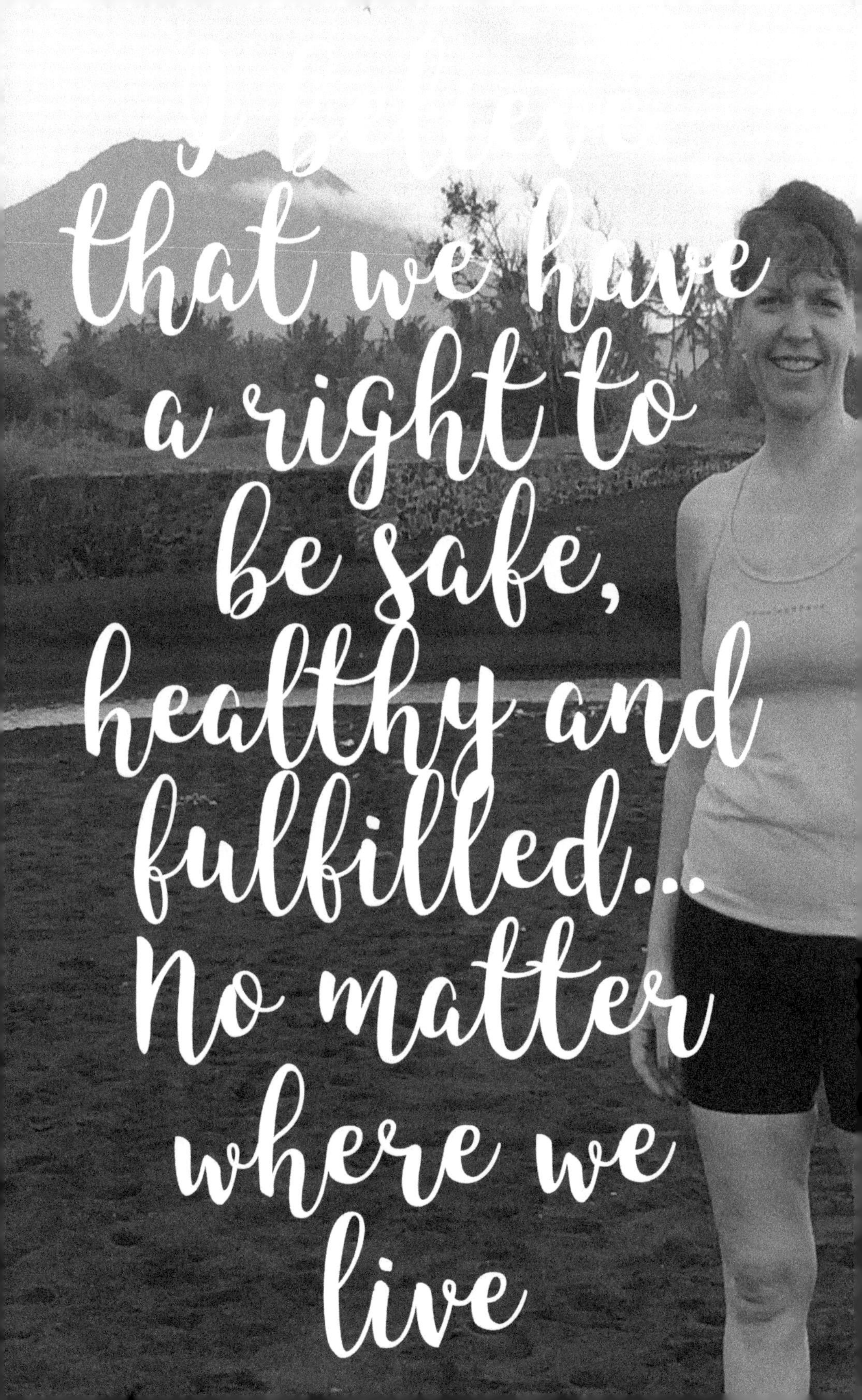

that we have
a right to
be safe,
healthy and
fulfilled...
No matter
where we
live

Chapter Five

There are a number of factors that impact the way that we approach food. We use food to both reward ourselves and also to punish ourselves. Much of the approach that we take with food is developed in childhood and we need to understand ourselves fully to work out how to change this. I talked about the development of your sense of self in Chapter One - this will also impact how you approach food.

A lot of the reason that we use food as comfort is because we don't feel good about ourselves. We often fall back on addiction pathways when this happens - and this is where food factors in, as it is the easiest thing to fall back on and we learn to do this as children.

Fat and sugar in equal proportions are, in combination, the most addictive substance for the brain. It is no surprise when we consider that biscuits, cake, chocolate and ice-cream all contain almost equal parts of fat and sugar.

As children, we learn our approach to food; often this approach is passed down from our parents. We usually teach our children that FOOD=COMFORT and, as an adult, this is a rather difficult connection to break.

It also gives us some insight into why people who develop other eating disorders, such as anorexia, are still utilising the comfort potential that comes from food but, instead of seeing it as a reward, they use it to punish themselves by withholding comfort. We need to understand this about ourselves to understand why it is **so** hard to impose a specific

DIET in our lives. If you are not in a really good emotional place, you cannot possibly look at making the rigid changes that are necessary to reduce your caloric intake.

@Food Awareness

Please now go to the website and in the 'Resources' area I want you to locate the document called 'Food Awareness'. You need to follow the instructions in this document carefully.

Take time completing this document and ensure that you prepare for the change you are going to make in your life by being really honest with yourself here. When you have completed this process you should note your observations in your 'Revolutionary Roadmap'.

Let me give you some insight…

My Yo-Yo Dieting Days

I have lost a lot of weight over the course of my life. I've also gained a lot. I have been a yo-yo dieter most of my adult life, but I have had a weight issue since I was a child. I remember being 'weighed and measured' at school - we had to line up in our underwear with all the other kids in our year and the nurse took measurements and read them out aloud, to be recorded on our school file. I recall this being quite a traumatic event for me in Year 3 as I was quite tall and I have a large frame for a woman. As it turned out I was the second heaviest girl in the class… And the heaviest girl was the 'fat girl'! I'm not trying to be nasty here, but I wasn't known as a 'fat kid' until then, because I carried my weight well. I still weigh more than most people think.

I was the youngest of five children with a sole parent mother - I grew up in poverty. We had staples that were carbohydrate based; it was rare that we had a lot of meat - when we did, it was usually sausages or mince. We didn't have a lot of money for sweets, but if we had dessert, we would have things like creamed rice - starch and sugar. We were active kids, riding our bikes around the neighbourhood - but we didn't have a lot of money for extracurricular activities. I did do calisthenics for a few years and I was good at it, but I lost interest when a new girl came in and took my leadership role in the troupe.

Food is strongly linked with emotion...
Love, Anger, Pain, Fear and Shame!

My weight fluctuated over the course of my childhood, depending on what was happening in my home. In my late primary school years, Mum was working full time in a childcare centre and she would bring home the excess milk for my brothers to drink - they were growing teenage boys. She would buy chocolate topping so they would drink the milk and not let it go to waste. However, I was the one who would come home to an empty house after school, and I quickly learned to comfort eat away my loneliness… Flavoured milk was a favourite for many years.

It was not until I was in my 30s that I was able to work out the link between the emotional feeling of loneliness and the desire for flavoured milk. It was a major issue for me in my weight loss journey - and I had to spend quite a bit of time in reflection to understand the desire and then undertake some therapy around the link to disconnect it.

The major weight gains and losses over the course of my life can clearly be tied to my emotional circumstances. I used to believe that I ate when I was happy and content, but I could also eat when I was sad and down. My best control over my eating was when I could externalise the focus of my weight loss goals. Funnily enough, this often meant that I would lose weight as I neared the end of a relationship. When I decided I wanted to take more control of my life and circumstances, I would often use my partner in a negative way to drive the control around my food intake. I saw it as a way of regaining my personal power.

However, I would begin a new relationship and become content for a while and the weight would start to creep back on. So I continued to yo-yo like this right up until I was in my mid-30s… Gain 10kgs, lose 10kgs… Gain 20kgs, lose 20kgs… Gain 30kgs, lose 30kgs! I had significant losses, but I also had significant gains. In the end, I was just over it - I wanted to stop the yo-yoing! So I had surgery to fit a gastric-band in 2007 because I thought this would 'fix' it!

Initially, I lost about 16kgs in the first four to five months, then I plateaued and I stayed at this weight for a good six months. My gastric-band hadn't 'fixed' it at all. I was having some issues in my relationship at this time and I had started to take back my personal power, but I was also in the final stages of my psychology degree and I became more aware of my tendency to really allow my emotional state to fuel my appetite. So I began to pay more attention to how I was feeling in that moment, when I was seeking to eat the things that I knew weren't good for me.

You see, people who are overweight KNOW what they should be doing, but in that moment when the desire is really strong, they just don't care! So I started spending more time in full awareness around my food intake and I discovered some amazing things. I used food to reward myself for SO many things it was unbelievable - anything I really didn't like, didn't want to do or made me uncomfortable - I would reward myself to do it, usually with chocolate or ice-cream.

I made a decision at this time to also stop drinking cold drinks that weren't water! I gave exception to wine in social situations. However, I stopped having any form of soft drink and stopped drinking juices or flavoured milk. I even reduced my coffee intake - I had been 'rewarding' myself with up to five large lattes per day; that was over two litres of milk with 10 teaspoons of sugar!

I also started labelling how I was feeling and addressing the underlying feeling, rather than using food to comfort me through it. I started using other things as a reward, such as beauty treatments or massages - they were bigger milestones to be rewarded for, but I promised myself the reward and I indulged in it. I started seeing that when I had labelled food as reward, I was actually doing more harm to my body in the long term. The real reward was in feeling more energetic within my own body as I started to lose more weight. However, until I had worked this out for myself, I was never going to make the adjustments to my eating habits that were needed in order to achieve significant weight loss.

It just so happened that my relationship ended around this time, but I really felt quite powerful and finally in control of my intake. I was on a steady decline in my weight, losing up to one kilogram per week. It was unusual because my relationship had ended on a rather strange note and I couldn't work out exactly what had gone wrong. This time, instead of feeding my hurt and confusion, I was able to sit with it and work through it… Until I found out the real reason for the demise of my marriage.

Three months after separating from my husband, I met with a girlfriend for lunch. I was explaining how I was moving through the financial settlement process and I was being very accommodating. My girlfriend decided I was being too accommodating, so she told me that my husband had been having an affair for most of that year with a much younger woman in his employ. Apparently, the only reason she hadn't told me earlier was because around the time she had decided to tell me, I had told her about the separation. However, she believed I was being manipulated in the financial negotiations and she wanted me to be aware of the real reason that my marriage failed.

This is the FIRST time in my life when emotions have rendered me **unable** to eat! I felt that I had been made to look like a fool, manipulated, lied to and I felt like I should have known better. In reality, I had suspected the affair but I had always been told that I was being ridiculous. As a result of this extreme emotional state, I lost my appetite… And I lost 15kg over the next three months! It took me that long to process the emotion and work through the issues. In the end, I was approaching the point where my weight loss was going too far and I forced myself to start taking better care of myself and my weight plateaued again.

I have maintained this lower weight, within about 5kgs, ever since. I no longer rigidly restrict myself, I eat pretty much whatever I want in smaller portions and I make adjustments to my diet when I notice that I have put on a few kilos. I regularly exercise and I do yoga, dance for fun and try to get outside and walk, run, cycle - whatever is fun. I see exercise as maintenance for my weight, but it also positively impacts my overall health and wellbeing.

I am more aware of how my emotions impact my desire for food, and I make adjustments for that - without judgement.

Nature or Nurture

If you grew up in a household in which your parents and/or siblings were overweight, there is often a strong sense that many of us feel that we just inherited bad genes. My mother used to talk about being big-boned and I was just big-boned like the rest of the family. However, we also know that the obesity epidemic has become much more of an issue in cultures where the onset of longer working hours for females means that we have a greater reliance on processed foods. There has been a steady increase in overall BMI in western cultures over the past 50 years.

Is there ANY evidence that your genetics impact on the development of weight issues? The short answer is yes. Genetics do play a part… But there is often an additional issue that flicks the switch in the genetic pathway. Interestingly, that switch is the impact of extreme stress.

@Twin Studies

There are a number of twin studies that have been conducted; one of the most interesting was done by Dr Tim Spector of King's College in London. He was studying the genetic differences in identical twins in which one had developed a weight issue and the other one had not. What he found, in a nutshell, was that there seems to be an obesity switch that is activated by extreme stress (see the video in the 'Resources' area on the website).

The next question we need to ask is - Is it what the stress hormones DO to the physical body, or is it the over-eating that humans tend to do when under stress, that causes the development of obesity? This is a more difficult question to answer, as it would require significant years of study and the detailed observation and recording of caloric intake over many years. So we are left to draw our own conclusions.

It is important to understand that we physically respond to stress as this affects our appetite and the way that we eat. This can be by over-eating, but also by under-eating. I know that when I am unhappy, I tend to over-eat - it is a comfort eating response. However, when I feel that I have had an experience that made me feel stupid, or that I should have known better, then I tend to stop eating as I lose my appetite and often experience somatic symptoms - like feeling nauseous.

So we can understand that stress has a significant impact on our food intake. So what? How do you then manage it? The key is in awareness… We need to be very careful to understand ourselves and our bodies, especially where food is involved. We can make much better food choices, but this is almost impossible if you are feeling very low. If you take this to the next level, we may see why we often put on weight in winter.

The Seasons and Food Intake

Winter - the colder weather and reduced light may lower our mood and we tend to comfort eat our way through winter. In addition, it can be difficult to maintain a good exercise regime. As a result, we tend to put on a little bit of weight and this can fuel negative feelings about ourselves, fuelling a downward spiral process, which lowers our mood even further.

Spring - you will notice a distinct improvement in mood as the days start to get longer again. We are exposed to more light and we see the life force in flowers blooming. Our mood will often naturally affect our appetite and we will start to eat less, especially less calorie dense food. Most people decide they need to do something about their weight at this point, to be ready for summer.

Summer - it is so much easier to eat lighter in summer. We often have celebrations though and we need to be mindful of those. In Australia, December marks the onset of summer, along with all of the Christmas preparations - drinks and parties. In general, we often gravitate towards salads and meat on BBQs and fresh fruit is usually plentiful. We naturally drink more water, which flushes the system and helps to move excess fat out of the body.

Autumn/Fall - as we say goodbye to the warmer weather, we can note the changes in colours and the tendency to look for more hearty foods. Often your mood doesn't take a total downward slide until the last month of autumn and then the colder weather really starts to impact mood.

Being aware of how the weather impacts our mood can be an important key in accepting that our physical self may fluctuate naturally and that we need to be aware, without judgement, of the changes and work out how to manage these changes without losing an overall sense of ourselves.

Eating in Full Awareness

Like with stress - my awareness around myself, how I'm feeling and what is fuelling those feelings, has a strong impact on how well I manage my food intake. When I am really clear about what is going on in my life, and I am being honest with myself, I can be more proactive in managing my food intake. If I have a day in which I walk in the door after work and I feel that I want to stuff my face with a block of chocolate and polish off a bottle of wine (we all have days like this sometimes!) I am now more aware and can engage in some preventative damage control.

I am a chocoholic - this is something I know about myself. So I will **always** allow myself to eat chocolate, because if I force myself NOT to indulge my driving desire for chocolate, I will make my desire stronger and before long, I have given myself some justification to feed it and then I tend to explode in over-indulgence.

So, I will always allow myself chocolate. As a result, I usually have one or two rows of dark couverture chocolate most evenings (20-40gms) and I take the time to enjoy it - I savour it, eat it slowly, and let it melt in my mouth. However, I have had days where I wanted to cram the block into my mouth - and some days I have just gone with it! The difference with my approach these days is that I won't allow myself to feel guilty about it... I am in complete awareness of what I am doing. I accept that, for whatever reason, this is the only way that I can cope with the situation I am in. I am in full acceptance of my behaviour and I am okay with it.

I don't take this approach every day, as I would not be in full awareness. It is also not an approach that I actively encourage in myself. I have spent years learning a range of diversion and stress management techniques. I often try many other things, but there are times when you just have to do it! The key difference for me now though - I WILL NOT judge and admonish myself for it. I am in loving acceptance of myself, aware that it was just what needed to be done at that time.

This is the ABSOLUTE KEY to changing the way you approach food in your life...

No Judgement

Full Acceptance

Total Awareness

Total awareness is where it becomes really interesting... Because if I am in total awareness of myself, I can accept that I will want to scoff my face on chocolate from time to time, sometimes as a direct behavioural result of an emotional response to a particular trigger. But it also means that I need to be aware that I cannot live my life in this way. In other words, you can't take this approach to food every day and just excuse it and accept it. Total awareness means that you have to face up to the source of your stress, and if it is a constant source, then it needs to be addressed.

It is often through dissatisfaction in the other areas of our lives - self, relationships, and career - that much of the feelings that feed our desire to eat really develop. This is why I say that the first thing you need to address in your life is your sense of self, as it holds the key to unlocking the behaviours that affect everything else in your life.

I am often impacted by relationships, and sometimes these can be working relationships. There can be stressful periods in a work environment that will leave your appetite emotionally affected. Awareness about those stressors means that you can make a temporary adjustment regarding the current situation, knowing that it has a limited life. Alternatively, you may need to make some decisions about removing yourself from certain situations if there appears to be no end in sight. This is why I say *total awareness*, because we need to be aware of how our environment is affecting us. If it is not positive, then we need to make changes - you cannot just feed yourself through it.

This is also true of intimate relationships. One of the big things that I am aware of is that I can put on weight in relationships because I am happy and content, but more often the greatest weight gains have happened when I am feeling unhappy. When the relationship is coming to an end, I often lose weight because by this time, I am more aware of my unhappiness in the relationship and I am planning my exit. As a result of taking control of my life by formulating a plan for the future, I am more content within myself and am able to eat better. I have already made my decision and I'm just working through the process.

As I have grown in my self-awareness, this process doesn't occur at the speed and volume that it used to. I now fluctuate within a 3-5kg window - not the 20-30kg range I used to operate in! The lack of judgement, and resulting acceptance, also means that I no longer compound my unhappiness by mindlessly over-eating, putting on weight, feeling bad about that and feeling powerless about my inability to control my impulses, which results in me wanting to overeat the pain away and slide into a large chasm of never-ending self-loathing and punishment… The slippery slope to obesity.

I talk a lot about 'mindful eating' and we need to understand the concept and learn how to take this approach to food. But at this point I want you to just stay with the concept that what you are putting in your mouth at any given moment is about that moment - not the rest of your day, week, month or year. This goes back to the concept of why we always say we will start the diet **tomorrow**…

We seem to take the approach that says if I over indulged at morning tea by eating biscuits or a chocolate bar - then I have blown the whole day and I should just give up. In this way, we are constantly undermining our efforts by throwing the baby out with the bath water!

Alternatively, if we take an approach to food that is everything in moderation and as feels necessary, our whole approach to food would change. There are a number of practical things that we need to put in place to do this, and I will give you some practical advice, but the reality is that most of you ALREADY know all there is to know about what you SHOULD be doing, you just find justification in your lives to avoid doing it.

But I 'deserve' it!

This is probably one of the most overused sentences in modern culture. We are so used to having to reward ourselves for doing the things that we find difficult, that we have developed into a society that uses food as reward.

We celebrate with food…

We console ourselves with food…

We use food to HEAL all wounds…

We show care with food…

We use food as punishment…

Food is usually at the centre of everything we do as human beings in 'commune' with one another. Weddings, anniversaries, funerals, births and birthdays… As human beings we always come together and socialise over food.

As parents we use food as reward, comfort and punishment. Hurt yourself? Here - have a biscuit while Mum cleans it up. Want ice-cream? Eat all your dinner first. Did something wrong? Go to your room without dinner! Food is such an integral part of our social interaction that we cannot pretend that we can just 'avoid' it.

Food is strongly linked with emotion - love, anger, pain, fear and shame!

Is it any wonder that we struggle to manage what is a sufficient intake? This notion is as applicable to under-eating as it is to over-eating. Those members of our society who would not be considered to have a weight problem are often people who have grown up using food as punishment. They see their ability to abstain as some sort of testament to their strength of character and may judge others who manage their food differently as being **weak** by comparison.

Of course, in case you hadn't realised… The key problem here is once again - Judgement!

The Exercise Myth

I'm not going to lie - exercise is important and an essential ingredient to long term weight management. However, it is not the key to weight loss. Quite the opposite… In fact, it is often a trigger for weight gain. Many of us decide we want to lose weight, so we join a gym. An interesting phenomenon can then occur, as the action that we take to achieve an outcome doesn't directly produce the desired result. The **purchase** of the membership doesn't create the weight loss… We still have to work at it! Most people who have weight issues hate the gym and most of us find an excuse NOT to go there, despite the expensive gym membership card in your wallet.

Good intentions do not equal great results.

The greatest weight loss will not come from exercise anyway. In fact, if you are not in the right mindset when you commence a new eating regime (I don't want to use the dirty D word), you will just end up using food to reward yourself for going to the gym and all of your hard work in exercising will be lost.

There have been numerous studies[7][8][9] that show that the commencement of a gym program can lead to weight gain because our brains justify the 250gm block of chocolate as a *reward* for going to the gym. Such a process cannot be sustained. The key to understanding how exercise plays a part in managing weight is to be clear that it needs to come into your life as something that is not hard to do. If it is too difficult, we will just avoid it and this is counterproductive.

So, the focus here is to try and give some thoughtful consideration to the kind of movement that you ENJOY! For me, I love to dance. So when I first started doing exercise in combination with my changed eating regime, I looked to things like belly dancing as a fun way to be active. In addition, I had always wanted to try yoga, so I also started attending a yoga class each week and then began to incorporate some yoga movements into my everyday morning routine.

I like to walk my dogs - so I make extra time to do that and I make it about them. Walking the dogs after work in the early evening achieves two key things - it allows you to de-stress and it serves to minimise the

7 https://www.ncbi.nlm.nih.gov/pmc/articles/PMC3771367/

8 https://www.ncbi.nlm.nih.gov/pmc/articles/PMC3044163/

9 https://www.ncbi.nlm.nih.gov/pmc/articles/PMC3862452/

overeating you often feel like doing in the evening. It also keeps you out of the fridge for an extra hour or so.

For me, I needed to find exercise regimes that I really enjoyed, so that I didn't have to REWARD myself to engage in them. When I initially lost weight, I didn't do much more than walk the dogs regularly and I took up belly-dancing for fun. But the real result came from being able to reduce my food intake, coupled with a few tricks and tips that have stayed with me over time and became part of my daily eating regime.

I DO NOT diet anymore... The concept is totally counterproductive.

I have adopted some standard food consumption practices into my life and I stick to them loosely. When I'm on holidays, I eat whatever I want and I deal with any resulting weight gain when I get back into my usual routine. I commenced regular organised exercise in a gym quite late in my weight loss process and then I joined a gym for women that offered a continuous circuit class. Quite quickly, I was exercising five days a week and this had been completely unheard of in my life prior to this time - and it was *effortless*. There was only one reason this really worked for me; I prioritised my attendance at the gym over other obligations - for once I actually put my own needs first, even though this felt selfish. I was able to do this and still work around my obligations to work and family.

There were other reasons that made this type of exercise more appealing, such as the fact that it was a continuous circuit - so I didn't have time to get bored. In addition, it had no set class times... For me this was the final barrier to all of my previous gym excuses. You see, previously, in other gym scenarios (and there had been many), I would always decide which classes I was going to attend that week and if something happened and I got delayed I would often decide NOT to go because I had missed that class. I would then need to wait for the same class the following week! This was a perpetuating cycle. By going to a gym that had no set class times, it didn't matter what time I went, I could always get a workout done so I had NO excuse... So I went, most days.

This exercise regime allowed me to enjoy my life without having to think about my food intake at all... That was such a relief. It also gave me access to a new social group as I met many regulars in the gym and I used to look forward to seeing them. This added to the appeal as I had a social connection there as well.

Over time, things changed and I've since ramped up my exercise routine another notch and joined another gym that is more physically demanding. For me, this is now about enhancing my physical capacity and improving my overall wellbeing, not really for weight loss purposes but for other health reasons.

This just goes to show that as our lives change and we adjust to our new routines, our motivation for engaging in different activities changes too, as does our ability to prioritise them. I have set new goals for myself that include taking up salsa dancing and engaging in more outdoor types of activities; things that allow me to get some great exercise and are also really good fun.

@The Plan

Please log in to your 'Membership' portal once again and download the document called 'My Plan'. Complete this now and note your result in your 'Revolution Roadmap'.

I have outlined for you the things that don't work, and the things that are counter-productive. Only you know yourself and your lifestyle, so in this plan we are going to develop a strategy that is unique to you and your weight loss journey.

You are Dedicated…
You are Divine!

Dharma Diva

Let's consider spirit and connection...

[illegible] that
energy flows
between people
and all
around us...
We can choose
how that
energy feels
and flows

Chapter Six

Have you ever gone on a spiritual exploration? Most people I know have spent some time in their life questioning the spiritual side of life - either due to the nature of their upbringing and the family belief system that has been imposed on them, or due to some form of personal 'search for meaning' at some time in their lives.

One of the things my mother used to say is that when things got very bad in her life, when she felt abandoned, lost and alone - she felt that she HAD to adopt a belief in God, or some form of external force with greater knowledge, power and infinite wisdom about her life - as she needed to believe that there was something out there that had full knowledge of her situation and would be able to get her through the difficult periods.

We often fall back on the need for a 'higher being' when we feel that things are very difficult in our lives - when we experience some level of trial and tribulation. From an individual psyche perspective, we focus on the belief that there must be something *greater* when we feel abandoned, when our interpersonal relationships fail us. We often feel so adrift in comparison to those around us that we believe that only a higher power could help us and then, only if we 'bargain' with it. Why is that?

Is this the last bastion of self?

If we take a religious rather than a spiritual view of this approach, then we come to see that this higher power can be everything from loving and merciful to judgemental and punishing and the difference is often just in the perspective taken by the individual.

If we take a spiritual perspective, we often see that the 'higher self' is just a state of consciousness and connection between all living creatures, in that it is a manifestation of the energy within us all. Depending on the level of insight, there can be a sense that we are all part of a continuous process of energy flow - positive and negative. Within that, there is also a realisation that the traditional notions of 'heaven and hell' are actually within us. For most people, they can look back over different times in their lives and understand this concept.

Who Am I?

Atheist, Agnostic, Hindu, Buddhist, Muslim, Christian, Fundamentalist? Somewhere in between? There are times when I have contemplated whether my own religious history is relevant to this chapter, but I think it is important to understand my journey and link it to how I have come to the space in which I now sit and how that may relate to the journey of others.

I was born into a Catholic household, the youngest of five children. My mother was a good Catholic and my father must have made some level of conversion for the purposes of marriage as they were married in a Catholic church and all of the children were baptised in the Catholic tradition. However, my parents initially sent my siblings to a public school.

It was after my father walked out on us that my mother decided that if there was *no* God, then she was screwed. She didn't believe that she could ever make it through that situation on her own. As a result, she started going to Mass every week and taking all five of us along. I'm not sure how renewed her vigour was in comparison to her attendance prior to my Dad leaving, but her commitment to regular religious services and the incorporation of Christian beliefs and practices in our home has continued throughout her life, although not necessarily in the same religious stream. This devotion had its impact on me.

Children learn what they live. I learned to believe in a loving and nurturing God, but I also had some experience with a spiritual connection - initially through the catechist movement in the Catholic Church and later through the Pentecostal movement. At one point in my life I had very strong ties to Christianity and lived my life accordingly. However, there was one burning issue that continued to plague me and it came to a head for me around the age of 20.

I believed in a loving and merciful higher power who was to be the ultimate 'Judge' of my behaviour and how I chose to live my life. I believed that I would need to account for that when this body no longer held life. However, at this time in my life, as a regular church attendee, what I was experiencing was a continuous sense of judgement from a lot of other people within these contexts. So much so, that I never felt accepted for ***who*** I was and constantly felt that I had to pretend to be someone else - I always felt like a fraud!

So, when I reflected on the judgement I was feeling, and my own understanding of the God I had been raised to believe in, I decided that I didn't need to subject myself to the judgement of those who said one thing and did another. I rejected the religious system; because for me the system was an active demonstration of hypocrisy.

I turned my back on organised religion, but maintained a level of connection to the awareness of a higher power, a moral base for interaction with the world and a sense of the energetic interaction of all life on the planet. I spent a good deal of my 20s having nothing to do with organised religion. When my own marriage failed and I was struggling with my own sense of self, I went back to church for a while but I reached the same conclusion again. It was the judgement I disagreed with, something I continue to disagree with to this day.

Judgement – Fundamentalism vs Acceptance

When we look at where disagreements manifest in this world, there is always judgement involved. The unrest that is publicised by news services across the globe is always due to the differences between groups, or the individuals who belong to particular groups, and the disagreement that develops when they hold different perspectives about life.

In psychology we talk about group dynamics, the sense of belonging that we get from feeling that we belong to a particular group. These groups can range from families, to schools and universities, through to community groups that come together for a shared purpose. Conflict develops where one group judges another group and believes that they are better than them.

At the most basic level, it happens between sporting groups. We play with or support a team, and they compete against another group to show who is better at a particular activity. This competition is often seen as a leisure activity, used to demonstrate the effectiveness of one group's skills in a game when directly compared to another group's skills. However, there is a whole lot of social interaction going on around these types of activities and they strongly reflect human behaviour in other areas of life.

You know when people talk about football, how some people openly admit that their dedication to it is 'like a religion'? It's absolutely true. This helps us to understand how some sporting events, such as football matches, have ended in riots and other hugely negative outcomes. We can extend the analogy to the whole of society, for a wide variety of different groups, but in the end, the contention can only develop through judgement.

If there is one thing I wish for in this world, it would be that we all seek to live our lives minimising judgement. If we did this across the globe - then there would truly be world peace.

I have even written about this in other books. In my contribution to "Better Business, Better Life, Better World" (https://www.amazon.com/Better-business-life-world-ebook/dp/B01MQOSO9W) I talk about the fact that if I could change one thing in this world it would be to eliminate unnecessary judgement.

Spiritual Search

I would not say that I actively went on a spiritual search, but something happened after I turned 40. According to René Allendy, a 19th century French psychoanalyst and homeopath who wrote a book called *"Le Symbolisme des Nombres"* or in English *"The Symbolism of Numbers"*, the number 40 *"is the achievement of a cycle in the world, or rather the rhythm of the cyclic repetitions in the Universe."*

I'm not going to enter into a debate about numerology. Pythagoras is the true father of numerological studies and education and I can't begin to compare with his insight and knowledge. Suffice to say that I believe there are numerical patterns in our lives and I have alluded to them earlier in this book when I discussed the developmental phases of life over seven year cycles.

Now 40 is an interesting number from a spiritual perspective; there are many references to it in a range of spiritual texts including the Bible and the Qur'an. It corresponds to the thirteenth Hebraic letter, mem, and to the Arcane 13 of the Tarot: The Death, marking the completion of a stage.

I believe that turning 40 is a life milestone that creates a fundamental shift within our being. For me, I decided that I wanted to explore a number of things at this point. My children were almost fully grown, I had more time to interact with different activities and I had finished my studies, so I had more time to 'explore'.

I travelled around Europe and also spent time in the USA and in parts of Asia. I spent time in churches and mosques, temples and ashrams, really for the buildings. I was more drawn to the architecture than any particular sense of religious or spiritual connection. To me, they are beautiful buildings dedicated to worship, and they all have different rituals around them, but they did not represent anything more to me than that.

East meets West: India or China?

I find it rather fascinating that two of the world's most ancient cultures, India and China, actually have similar 'systems' for ordering things in life. Seemingly independently (although I'm sure there were travellers between them who passed through the Himalayas) both cultures developed a similar set of concepts almost 5000 years ago. These systems are still very relevant today. Both cultures focus on the following five areas of life:

Astrology – Jyotish or Chinese Horoscopes

Space Design – Vaastu Shilpa or Feng Shui

Physical Activity – Yoga or Tai Chi

Medicine – Ayurvedic Medicine or Traditional Chinese Medicine

Five Universal Elements – Ayurveda and Wu Xing

Energy Systems

They also have an understanding of the energy systems in the body. In India they talk about chakras and in China they talk about meridians;

in essence they are both looking at the same thing - the energy system and how it flows within our bodies. Modern western medicine talks about these as 'nodes' and they are present in our body and are affected by a range of emotions and they can be adjusted with food, herbs, medicines and physical movement.

There are seven chakras and the meridians surround these. In essence, they relate to the following areas of our lives:

Base – Security

Sacrum – Sexuality

Belly – Home and Community

Heart – Family and Relationships

Throat – Communication

Forehead – Insight

Top of the Head – Spiritual Connection

Spirit – Isn't it all the same anyway?

Ashrams are quite different to other buildings dedicated to spiritual pursuits – there is not a sense that the physical building is important, but more that the activities that are performed within it are what is important. Perhaps this is what drew me more towards yoga rather than other spiritual pursuits. Apart from anything else, the thing I most like about yoga and the yogic lifestyle is that it is completely open to whatever spiritual beliefs you choose to have. Essentially, because it is based in Hinduism, there is an acceptance of multiple deities within yoga. There is also a general acceptance of a whole range of things…

So what is yoga? Yoga is…

- A union between the individual and the cosmic self
- A universal science of self-discovery, which evolved from the lifestyle and practices of the ancient seers
- A comprehensive and practical system of transforming the human personality, which leads to balanced development of physical health, mental harmony and spiritual upliftment
- A lifestyle that can change the quality of body and mind, allowing us to understand and fulfil our true potential

My Thoughts

A sense of spiritual
connection allows
you to uplift
yourself and
everyone around
you, in true
self-awareness...
Each expression,
Each thought, Each
sentiment conveys
an intuitive wisdom

Kerry Howard

- A positive way to enhance our creativity and expression in life through the unfolding of deeper dimensions of consciousness
- A system that has a unique and universal appeal and may be practised by people from all walks of life, on all continents and of all religions
- A practical philosophy which can create better human conditions and situations around the globe

Vision Australasia (2011), Satyananda Yoga Academy

Not just the Physical

Modern life has shown us yoga in many forms in our society, most of them about the area of yoga referred to as the 'Asanas' - the physical postures. The awareness and skills developed through the practice of yoga should extend beyond the mat into all levels and conditions of life. The application of yogic principles helps you to develop a more balanced and integral lifestyle, and to stand on your own two feet.

The appeal to me of this type of approach to life is that in this space you are able to assume responsibility for yourself in all situations and respond in ways that are constructive and appropriate. Yoga teaches you to become much more self-aware. As a result, when living a more self-aware life, you are able to engage in relationships and life events with a clearer perspective, without becoming caught-up.

In awareness you also improve your relationships, as you are able to understand the problems and difficulties of others, you develop a healthy sense of empathy and know clearly how to help and support those around you. In this way, a sense of spiritual connection allows you to uplift yourself and everyone around you. When you adopt this style of approach in true self-awareness, each expression, each thought, each sentiment conveys an intuitive 'wisdom'.

As you have read through this book, you can see how it is that my vision and self-awareness really started to merge when I found yoga. I love engaging in the physical postures; they make me feel relaxed and clear and assist me to manage some of my physical issues, the injuries that have developed over the course of my life.

However, I also really enjoy spending time in the ashram, living the embodiment of what yogic tradition encourages, away from the confines of judgement… This really is an empowering experience. It allows me to connect with the spiritual aspect of myself, but in a way that feeds and nurtures my system. Time in the ashram provides renewal, vigour and an energetic cleansing process that I have found to be a lovely addition to my life.

But I do not want this book to 'preach' yoga at you… Far from it! That's not what yoga does and certainly not what I intend. As individuals, we need to find some level of spiritual connection that feeds our soul and gives our lives purpose. Prior to my contact with yoga, I had opportunity to read the book *'Big Mind, Big Heart'* by Zen Master, Dennis Genpo Merzel. I encourage you to read his work and, if nothing else, listen to the radio interview that comes with his book. I provide the link to it in the Resources area on the website.

Time – Elements

The seven-year development cycles also link to different elemental phases in our lives. When we look at texts like the I-Ching and the Tao, we come to understand how elemental forces closely link to these seven-year phases in our lives.

The Growth Cycles

Usually known as the Five Elements,[10] Chinese Taoist cosmology[11] Wu Xing is also known as the Five Movements, Five Phrases or Five Steps. The five elements are Jin (metal), Mu (wood), Shui (water), Huo (fire) and Tu (earth). The five elements in daily life were regarded as the foundation of everything in the universe and natural phenomena. They have their own characters and they can generate or destroy one other. These five elements are the basis of Chinese metaphysics and philosophy and have practical applications in feng shui, astrology and traditional Chinese medicine.

Generating Interaction (also begetting, engendering or mothering): Metal generates water; water nourishes wood; wood feeds fire; fire creates earth/ash; earth bears metal.

---

10 https://www.travelchinaguide.com/intro/astrology/five-elements.htm

11 http://susanlevitt.com/about/writers-resume/the-five-taoist-elements-fire-earth-metal-water-and-wood/

Overcoming Interaction (also destruction): Fire melts metal; metal chops wood; wood breaks up earth; earth absorbs water; water quenches fire.

Ayurveda explains that the entire cosmos or universe, including our bodily systems, is made up of five different types of materials; in Ayurveda they are called the Pancha-bhootas[12]. The first among them is Akash (ether/space) - which is all around us, then comes Vayu (air) - the gaseous material, next is Agni (fire) - which heats or transforms, fourth is Jal (water) - the liquid material and finally Prithvi (earth) - the solid material. They account for the five faculties of Shabda (sound), Sparsha (touch), Roopa (sight), Rasa (taste) and Gandha (smell). Thus every individual has these distinct five faculties as each of these faculties has emanated from one particular element. Another way of dividing the cosmos into elemental energies is the ancient East Indian vedic system of the three doshas: vata (air/space), pitta (fire), and kapha (earth and water). These three doshas are used in Ayurvedic medicine in a system as fully developed as traditional Chinese medicine.

You may be more familiar with the four elements of fire, water, air, and earth as these are the basis of many magical and spiritual systems including the four corners of pagan ritual, the four elements of alchemy, the native American medicine wheel and the four elements of astrology. Even the tarot deck and playing cards are based on these four elements whereby fire is wands (clubs), water is cups (hearts), air is swords (spades) and earth is pentacles (diamonds).

I will not attempt to begin to provide any level of in depth analysis or comparison between these or any other philosophies, I do not profess to be an expert in this area. You may like to explore www.indianscriptures.com further if you are interested in learning more. This site is a great resource and provides quite a lot of useful information and comparisons with other classification systems.

I liken the growth cycles to the Wu Xing in the following information, but there are elemental similarities to the process outlined in Ayurveda; in essence I think that we can apply a number of different elemental processes to growth, but I like the way the Wu Xing elements link to phases in the life cycle.

12 http://www.indianscriptures.com/vedic-lifestyle/beginners-guide/pancha-bhootas-or-the-five-elements

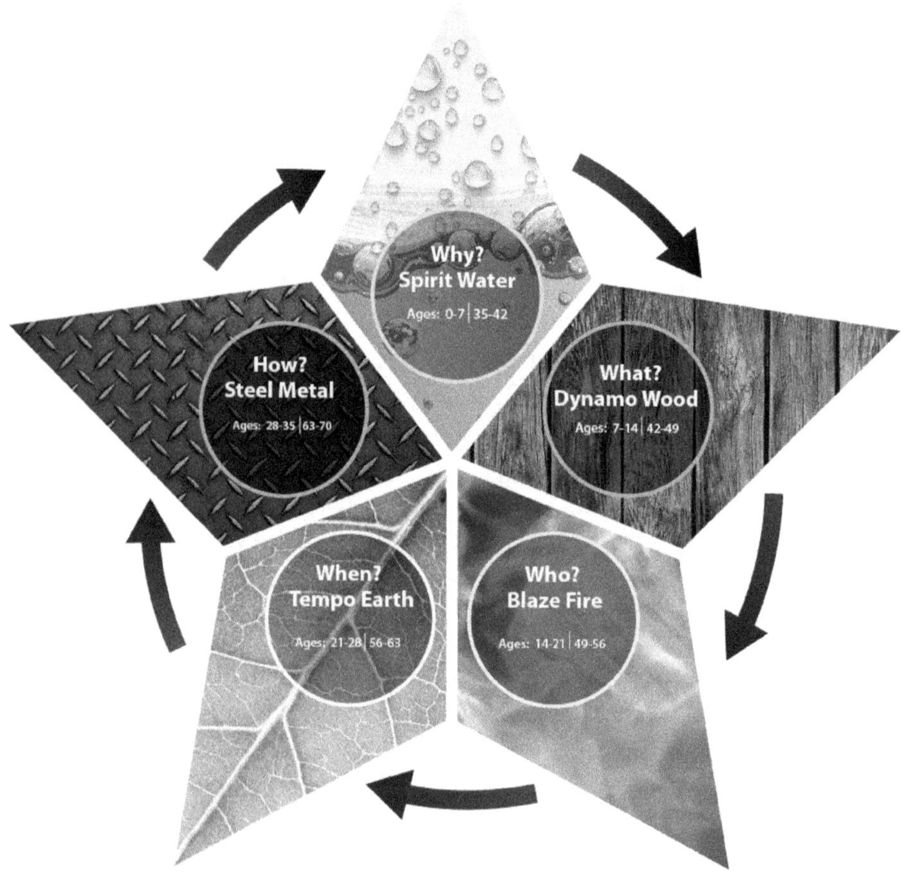

Water – Spirit

0-7 and 35-42

Characterised by wisdom, water pronounces the talent, sage or fool, representing aptitude, brightness, agile mind and accuracy.

Water is the most feminine of the five elements and therefore is considered very yin. In Taoist cosmology, femininity is not considered weak. On the contrary, water is the most powerful element for it can move around any obstacle in its path without losing its essential nature. Water can, in time, dissolve the hardest mountains.

Water qualities are creativity, sensitivity, reflection, persuasion, effectiveness, and desire for life and sex. Water values family and social contacts and possess the ability to attract rather than pursue. The emotion associated with water is fear, which creates indecisiveness and uncertainty.

The water phases in our lives are an awareness period - I often refer to the early phase, from birth until age seven, as the development of the root system in a tree, the forming of the foundation for growth. These are insightful times of learning in which we become consciously unaware, meaning that we become aware that there are things we do not know and this prompts a time of consideration for growth. This explains why we often start to question our life path and overall happiness after the age of 35.

Wood – Dynamo

7-14 and 42-49

Characterised by benevolence, wood pronounces the fate, lowliness or nobleness, representing extractive, luxuriant, brilliant, blooming and flourishing growth.

The wood element is masculine and considered less yang than fire. Wood's planet is Jupiter, the largest planet, symbolic of wood's growth in springtime. Wood's season is spring, the time of planting seeds, beginnings, and new growth. Wood's position represents ancestors and family relationships.

Wood qualities are bold actions, planning, initiating new projects, idealism, imagination, compassion, and competition. It's a time for decisive action and creating change. The emotion associated with wood is anger, which creates tension, criticism, discouragement, regret, excitement, dislike of self and others and negative judgement.

The wood phases in our lives are a foundational growth period - I refer to the early phase, from age seven until adolescence, as the development of the trunk and branches in the tree, the main structure or strength of the tree. These are times of growth in which we are consciously aware and trying to learn new things, changing, improving and often being frustrated in the process. This explains why we often experience a 'mid-life crisis' in our 40s, we are growing and changing and often getting frustrated with the limitations of our structures.

Fire – Blaze

14-21 and 49-56

Characterised by propriety, fire pronounces the feature, strength or softness, representing power, influence, bravery and intensity.

Fire is the most masculine of the five elements. Therefore it is considered very yang. Fire's planet is Mars, the intense red planet. Fire's season is summer, the time of heat, growth, warmth and increased light. Fire's position represents fame and illumination.

Fire qualities are love, passion, leadership, spirituality, insight, dynamism, aggression, intuition, reason and expressiveness. Fire is bold and forthright but also warm-hearted and generous. This phase is strongly linked to experiences of love, compassion, fun, joy and pleasure.

The fire phases in our lives are periods of independence and clarity. In the early phase, our adolescence from 14-21, it is a time of asserting our independence and working out who we really are. Fire is involved in the volatile heart emotions of jealousy, frustration, regret, grief from loss of love and disappointment in relationships. However, in our later years this tends to be a period of joy and happiness. Following on from the period in which we wish to redefine ourselves, the phase from 49-56 is often when we are truly accepting of ourselves, we can step into our 'true' selves and be secure in our unique value and enjoy it.

Earth – Tempo

22-28 and 57-63

Characterised by fidelity/honesty, earth pronounces the status, rich or poor, representing the birth and growth of everything.

Earth is yin, feminine, like Mother Earth in the West. Earth's planet is Saturn. Earth corresponds to all twelve earthly branches and its 'season' is the last eighteen days of each of the four seasons, the time of seasonal transition. Earth's location (direction) is the centre. Earth's position represents unity and balance. Earth's symbol is the yin/yang.

Earth qualities are sympathy or empathy, which can result in pensiveness, thoughtfulness and reflection. It is a time for assimilating our life experiences, helping to digest and accept fate and expand our circle of knowledge.

These are times of balance and settling to check the lay of the land. In our early phase it is often a time when we feel 'established' and clear in who we have decided to be. It is often when we settle down, setting clear boundaries and taking care of ourselves, a time when we have greater empathy for each other and honour others through our demonstration of kindness. In our later life it also represents a period in which we often feel quite settled and accepting of what we have done with our life.

Metal - Steel

29-35 and 64-70

Characterised by righteousness, metal pronounces the life span, longevity or abortion, foretelling any penalties, dangers, difficulties and dead ends.

This element is feminine because metal is extracted from the feminine earth, although metal is considered less feminine than earth or water. Metal's planet is Venus. Metal's season is autumn, the time of harvest, completion and the beginning of rest. Metal's direction is west and it correlates to children and creativity.

Although metal is a lesser yin element, it can exist in either a yang or a yin state. Metal qualities include strength, independence, focus, intensity, righteousness and fluency in speech; it can be determined and powerful. Metal can also be characterised by grief and this can lead to insecurity, inability to achieve expectations and lack of confidence.

These are times of mastery and completion. There is a sense of achievement in metal life phases, an awareness that things are slowing down, settled. Metal phases bring with them a sense of reaping the rewards, that feeling that 'I did it!' It is towards the end of metal phases that we start to question things as we move into the next phase of growth again, which begins in water.

Relax – Flow

As you can see from the life phases, it is not surprising that we have a mid-life review point where we need to make a significant adjustment to our life direction. A huge part of the ability to feel satisfied with where you are at in your life is about the ability to link into your life phase in awareness and see it as an opportunity to move with the 'flow', the natural rhythm of the universe and your current position within it.

Dance – More than Just Exercise

There are many forms of dance that have developed over many years in different cultures. Dance is also often noted in spiritual texts. Sufi Dervish and dance in spiritual expression, in some texts, are referred to as an ecstatic expression.

More recently, within the psychotherapy world, there are a number of people who are introducing dance in a therapeutic way. There are several schools of thought around this and many different teachers around the world, but it is clear to see that the ability to express emotion through movement is something that has had seasons of popularity over the generations in spiritual pursuits and more people should probably embrace it. Dance allows us to do a number of things including releasing physical tension in our bodies and getting in touch with our emotional state - but many people are unable to reduce their inhibitions for long enough to fully engage with it.

There is a more recent phenomenon, known as 'No Lights, No Lycra', that has developed in response to this issue. If you do some research you will likely find a group in your area. It is exactly what it says it is - a place for people to go and dance, in the dark where no one can see you. It doesn't matter how you dance, what you wear or anything else, it is a space without judgement and an opportunity to 'let go' and have fun through dance. There are no set movements, so you can just release yourself to the music and enjoy.

I have also done some ecstatic dance classes at the ashram. In this situation, you are part of a group of people who come with open minds and hearts and you close your eyes and move to the music in whatever way you feel to express yourself. It is amazingly cathartic and definitely creates energy and reinvigorates the body.

My Thoughts

Self-Reflection

It is really important that we learn to approach life with regular self-reflection. This is what helps us to maintain our awareness and get on top of any negative thinking that may arise in our lives.

Self-reflection is the best way to tap into the things that are not 'serving' us and gives us an opportunity to make different decisions about our future. Most of us have lived our lives in self-avoidance. We often look at things external to us and blame them for our unhappiness - in judgement. If every human being learned to spend time in self-reflection and develop awareness, then we would see great changes in our world.

@Desire Design

Please log in to your 'Membership' portal once again and download the document called 'Desire Design'. Complete this now and note your result in your 'Revolution Roadmap'.

Living Mindfully

Mindfulness as a concept is a much bigger issue than self, relationships, career, finances, health and wellbeing or spirit.

We need to briefly step back into the world where eastern philosophy meets psychotherapy. From the roots of Zen Buddhism, we find the core of mindfulness, which is 'meditating daily life'. It is about paying maximum attention, with all our senses, to the experience of the moment we are currently in. It is the idea that 'you only have moments to live' and that we live our lives moment by moment. If we are not present in the moment, not attending fully to the moment, then we are not really living our lives.

Rewarding and Replenishing

The other thing that we need to remember is that the feeling of happiness is assisted by positive experiences. It is in the 'experience' that you feel that life is worth living. We have developed a society of consumerism rather than experience, and this has provided a lot of fuel for our feelings of dissatisfaction.

Most of us seek to buy new things, but the sense of gratitude for items quickly wears off. The item quickly becomes part of our everyday world and the joy of the purchase fades. However, when you reflect on your experiences, places you have visited or people you have spent time with, these still bring a smile to your face and you never lose the joy of that experience.

I now spend a lot of time travelling. I have a house and it needs some renovation work, but my driving force for the allocation of my hard earned money is in travel. I love to experience new cultures - I mean REALLY experience them. Not just go and stay in a resort, but get out amongst the locals and see how they really live. This experience allows me to appreciate home more, but I am enriched for the experience and my ability to be able to imbibe some culture into my system from everywhere I travel.

In travel though, you really should approach it with an open heart. It is not our place to enter into another culture with judgement. I will often find situations in different countries 'amusing', but I do try very hard not to make that a judgement, more an observation of the difference and a curiosity about what prompts certain behaviours.

In this way I can see the wonderful and colourful differences in cultures and appreciate them for what they are. I never go to a new country and complain about the things that I have at home and why they are not also there. If I am really attached to those things, then I am better off just staying at home.

I have one particular story of standing in the main square in Florence, Italy. In front of me the most amazing sight - the Duomo and the Baptistery side-by-side, glorious buildings that are covered in small mosaic tiles - the whole building! I am standing in absolute awe of the craftsmanship in these buildings when in the back of my consciousness I become aware of another person's voice…

> *"Where's the Ben and Jerry's! I want Ben and Jerry's! They said there is a Ben and Jerry's in the square, but I don't see one! Why can't these Italians ever get anything right?"*

I admit, my initial reaction to this woman was anger, but then I checked myself and decided to try a softer approach. So I turned to her and said,

> *"You are in the home of gelato. There are at least a dozen gelataria around the square - beautiful handmade Italian ice cream. You can have Ben and Jerry's at any time whilst you are at home, perhaps you could just enjoy something different."*

My comment was initially greeted with stunned silence. The voice had come from one of three young women. After a brief pause she said *"But I don't eat any food that I don't know!" This outlines clearly where, for some people, the approach to 'experience' is completely lost.*

No Right or Wrong – Connection with the Self

The 'key' to true awareness and enlightenment from a spiritual connection is the ability to recognise that as human beings we all have an energy that is interconnected. If I give my positive energy to someone else, I do so in gratitude. However, I am also aware that I can only do so much of that before my own energy starts to become affected and I need to engage in activities that reenergise me.

As a therapist this is a key understanding that I have had to incorporate into my work. There are only so many hours in a working week that you can *give* before you need to 'replenish'. When people work in caring roles, and women often work in these areas, or even just in our family relationship roles where we are often the nurturers, at some point in time, if we give too much of ourselves without replenishing, then we run out of energy to give.

This is why the spirit aspect of this **re-LOVE-olution** is SO important…

You need to sort your life out, but then you need to live it mindfully, in full awareness, so that you can manage the 'ebbs and flows' of life. You need to LOVE yourself for all of the aspects that define you… Your true self.

This is why the title of this book is *'Define Your Inner Diva'* - because being a Diva is about being deliciously connected to life, a woman of outstanding talent who is committed to living life to its fullest capacity.

You are Delightful...
You are Delectable...
You are Decisive...
You are Discerning...
You are Divine...
You live Dharma...
You are Fempowered!

Welcome Diva

Epilogue

You have engaged openly and honestly in a process of true self-examination. You have faced up to the negative beliefs you held about yourself and been able to move through these, in understanding and acceptance of your true nature.

You can now stand in front of the mirror and LOVE the person that you are - if not 100% today, certainly more than you did when you started on this journey of self-discovery.

You have been able to see how your sense of self has impacted your relationships and you are able to be clear about who you are and what you bring to a relationship. You now know what you want and what you are prepared to compromise on, in return.

You are more aware of your career and working life and how this impacts on your sense of self. You have clarity about what you want for yourself in the future and you have a plan of action to move yourself forward, but with a softness of acceptance, you realise that you need perseverance and patience… With those, you will succeed.

You have a greater insight into your financial position and how you need to be more aware of what you want for yourself in the future and how you can take steps to ensure you have the resources you need into the future.

You have been able to see how your sense of self impacted your approach to your health and wellbeing, and even though change in this area may take a while to bear fruit, you can see how your current situation developed and you are more aware of the beliefs that keep you there.

Finally, you have examined your sense of spiritual connection and how it can be the source of reinvigoration, but also a place of balance. This is about how you manage your energy and keep yourself in a space of good balance - Yin/Yang - truly complementary.

Congratulations Gorgeous… You are Fempowered - an embodied Diva!

Ms Pink
XXX

Resources

If you prefer, or you would like additional copies, go to the website www.mspinkherself.com and go to the 'Resources' area and log into the 'Membership' portal that has been specially designed for people who have purchased this book. Here you will find all of the resources that accompany this book. Also, as a special extra for being a member of the clan, I will also periodically add additional resources that may be relevant to you in the future.

Chapter One - Self

@My Ten Things

@My Belief System

@Self Worth Inventory

@Strengths Assessment

Chapter Two – Relationships

@ Review of Behaviours

@Clarifying Our Needs

@DailyReflection

@Traits List

@Financial Agreement – Basic

Chapter Three – Career

@Personality Profile Assessment

@Future Template

Chapter Four – Finances

@Basic Financial Review

Chapter Five – Health and Wellbeing

@Food Awareness

@The Plan

Chapter Six – Spirit

@Desire Design

Appendix 1

NEGATIVE AND POSITIVE COGNITIONS

NEGATIVE	POSITIVE
Responsibility: Defective	
I don’t deserve love	I deserve love; I can have love
I am a bad person	I am a good (loving) person
I am terrible	I am fine as I am
I am worthless (inadequate)	I am worthy; I am worthwhile
I am shameful	I am honourable
I am not lovable	I am lovable
I am not good enough	I am deserving (fine/OK)
I deserve only bad things	I deserve good things
I am permanently damaged	I am (can be) healthy
I am ugly (my body is hateful)	I am fine (attractive/lovable)
I do not deserve…	I can have (deserve)
I am stupid (not smart enough)	I am intelligent (able to learn)
I am insignificant (unimportant)	I am significant (important)
I am a disappointment	I am OK just the way I am
I deserve to die	I deserve to live
I deserve to be miserable	I deserve to be happy
I am different (don’t belong)	I am OK as I am
Responsibility: Action	
I should have done something*	I did the best I could
I did something wrong*	I learned (can learn) from it
I should have known better*	I do the best I can (I can learn)

*What does this say about you?
(eg. does it make you feel:
shameful/stupid/like a bad person)

Safety/Vulnerability

I cannot trust anyone	I can choose whom I trust
I cannot protect myself	I can (learn to) take care of myself
I am in danger	It's over I am safe now
I am not safe	I am safe now
It's not okay to feel (show) my emotions	I can safely feel (show) my emotions

Control/Choices

I am not in control	I am now in control
I am powerless (helpless)	I now have choices
I am weak	I am strong
I cannot get what I want	I can get what I want
I cannot stand up for myself	I can make my needs known
I cannot let it out	I can choose to let it out
I cannot be trusted	I can be trusted
I cannot trust myself	I can (learn to) trust myself
I cannot trust my judgment	I can trust my judgment
I am a failure (will fail)	I can succeed
I cannot succeed	I can succeed
I have to be perfect (please everyone)	I can be myself (make mistakes)
I cannot stand it/I am inadequate	I am capable
I cannot trust anyone	I can choose whom to trust

Appendix 2

Negative Traits	Positive Traits
aggressive	adaptable
aloof	adventurous
arrogant	affable
belligerent	affectionate
big-headed	agreeable
bitchy	ambitious
boastful	amiable
bone-idle	amicable
boring	amusing
bossy	brave
callous	bright
cantankerous	broad-minded
careless	calm
changeable	careful
clinging	charming
compulsive	communicative
conservative	compassionate
cowardly	conscientious
cruel	considerate
cunning	convivial
cynical	courageous
deceitful	courteous
detached	creative
dishonest	decisive
dogmatic	determined
domineering	diligent
finicky	diplomatic
flirtatious	discreet
foolish	dynamic
foolhardy	easy-going
fussy	emotional
greedy	energetic
grumpy	enthusiastic

Negative Traits	Positive Traits
gullible	exuberant
harsh	fair-minded
impatient	faithful
impolite	fearless
impulsive	forceful
inconsiderate	frank
inconsistent	friendly
indecisive	funny
indiscreet	generous
inflexible	gentle
interfering	good
intolerant	gregarious
irresponsible	hard-working
jealous	helpful
lazy	honest
Machiavellian	humorous
materialistic	impartial
mean	independent
miserly	intellectual
moody	intelligent
narrow-minded	intuitive
nasty	inventive
naughty	kind
nervous	loving
obsessive	loyal
obstinate	modest
overcritical	neat
overemotional	nice
parsimonious	optimistic
patronising	passionate
perverse	patient
pessimistic	persistent
pompous	pioneering
possessive	philosophical
pusillanimous	placid
quarrelsome	plucky
quick-tempered	polite
resentful	powerful
rude	practical

Negative Traits	Positive Traits
ruthless	pro-active
sarcastic	quick-witted
secretive	quiet
selfish	rational
self-centred	reliable
self-indulgent	reserved
silly	resourceful
sneaky	romantic
stingy	self-confident
stubborn	self-disciplined
stupid	sensible
superficial	sensitive
tactless	shy
timid	sincere
touchy	sociable
thoughtless	straightforward
truculent	sympathetic
unkind	thoughtful
unpredictable	tidy
unreliable	tough
untidy	unassuming
untrustworthy	imaginative
vague	understanding
vain	versatile
vengeful	warmhearted
vulgar	willing
weak-willed	witty

About the Author

Kerry Howard, Ms Pink Herself, is passionate about helping people to experience their best life, even when they are not sure it is possible.

Kerry is a psychologist, executive coach, mother, daughter and definitive diva. She has worked with over 500 clients to improve their sense of self and find their joy in life. Kerry's book, *Define Your Inner Diva*, is a culmination of her life's work in the personal transformation space.

Kerry is also a charismatic keynote presenter. She draws on her own life experiences and practice to deliver powerful messages in a truly authentic way. She presents on a diverse range of topics including personal growth, relationships, weight loss, trauma and life transformation.

Put simply, Kerry provides profoundly simple insights that are changing the way thousands of women think about their careers and their lives.

Look out for Kerry's next book in early-2018

why men are like shoes

Why Men Are Like Shoes is an irreverent look at dating for women, using an analogy that most women understand - a love of 'shoes'.

Kerry is passionate about helping people to experience their best life, even when they are not sure it is possible, and that includes having fun with dating and relationships. Kerry has an absolute love of being able to assist people to turn their lives around.

"I get pure joy from being able to give somebody a different perspective of themselves and see them make significant change and truly believe it. It's wonderful to see that light bulb moment in their eyes, when they finally understand why they've been doing the same thing over and over and over again and why they don't have to do it anymore! It's awesome when an individual can start seeing themselves in a completely different way, really like who they are, and change their lives as a result."

You can 'Pre-Register' for your copy of Why Men Are Like Shoes by going to following link on the website. As a Diva, you will also receive an 'Extra Special BONUS' for pre-registering...

http://mspinkherself.com/why-men-are-like-shoes/

www.ingramcontent.com/pod-product-compliance
Ingram Content Group UK Ltd.
Pitfield, Milton Keynes, MK11 3LW, UK
UKHW020142250726
13967UKWH00002B/806